Stop the Pendulum

Stop the Pendulum

Public Policy and Personal Experience in Reading Instruction and Reform

William D. Bursuck and Craig Peck

ROWMAN & LITTLEFIELD
Lanham • Boulder • New York • London

Published by Rowman & Littlefield
An imprint of The Rowman & Littlefield Publishing Group, Inc.
4501 Forbes Boulevard, Suite 200, Lanham, Maryland 20706
www.rowman.com

86-90 Paul Street, London EC2A 4NE, United Kingdom

Copyright © 2022 by William D. Bursuck and Craig Peck

All rights reserved. No part of this book may be reproduced in any form or by any electronic or mechanical means, including information storage and retrieval systems, without written permission from the publisher, except by a reviewer who may quote passages in a review.

British Library Cataloguing in Publication Information Available

Library of Congress Cataloging-in-Publication Data Available

ISBN 978-1-4758-6391-8 (cloth) | ISBN 978-1-4758-6392-5 (pbk)
| ISBN 978-1-4758-6393-2 (electronic)

Contents

Preface		vii
1	Introduction	1
2	Teaching Reading 1955–1983: Instructional Disputes, Federal Involvement, and the Roots of Reform	17
3	Experiences: Teaching Reading in Urban and Rural Settings, 1968–1978	29
4	Teaching Reading 1983–2008: Reading Policy Takes Center Stage	51
5	Experiences: A Thirty-Year Career in Teacher Education, 1983–2013	67
6	Policy and the Personal: What We Learned from Seven Decades of Reading Instruction and Reform	91
References		107
About the Authors		111

Preface

Despite over fifty years of trying to solve it, the achievement gap in reading remains one of our country's most intractable problems. One of the cornerstones of our democracy—our public schools—has been hampered by a cornerstone failing: a chronic inability to help students who struggle academically become better readers. Consequently, just as our society is marked by dividing lines of class, race, and other demographic markers, so too are we divided into a nation of readers and those who are unable to read.

Our purpose in this project is to help shed light on this problem by providing a compelling, accessible history of reading instruction and school reform in the United States since 1955. While the search for the best method of teaching reading is centuries old, reading instruction only became part of public policy debates and actions in the final two decades of the twentieth century. During and since that time, the field of reading has undergone multiple internal struggles that continue to influence reading policy debates of today. As a result, reading instruction became and remains a central element in major educational policy and reform initiatives meant to transform and fundamentally improve American education.

As authors, we bring unique perspectives to this subject. Throughout our careers, each of us has served as K-12 educators and university researchers while at the same time engaging in school improvement activities that made us inevitably into school reformers. As both former practitioners and informed scholars, we are well-positioned to provide insights into reading instruction and school reform as they were in the past and as they are today.

In our book, we combine attention to describing the policy and practical history related to reading instruction and school reform with an intimate focus on the career of author Bill Bursuck, whose work in reading and school improvement has spanned over four decades. In this way, we focus on the personal, the practical, and the political in providing thoughtful, engaging insight into a central teaching issue of our times.

An admission upfront is that we are both diehard "middle of the roaders" in regard to our subject. For instance, we support what Gough and Turner (1986) called the *simple view of reading*. The simple view of reading recognizes that what to teach in beginning reading is not an either-or proposition. In this view, both decoding and reading comprehension are crucial skills to nurture in the beginning reader and both need to be taught systematically and explicitly. Decoding is taught early, but so is comprehension in the form of language comprehension skills.

We are also advocates for compromise and consensus-building as antidotes to the "reading wars." We endorse what Pearson calls "the radical middle," in which pragmatists like us search for common ground in shared, inclusive principles and ideas regarding reading instruction. Only by coming together ideologically can we close the achievement gap that too often divides us along various demographic lines.

So, who should read this book? Researchers who study the teaching of reading specifically and educational reform generally will find much of interest within these pages. Specifically, we anticipate that our account will make an important scholarly contribution by providing documentation of and insight into the political, social, and cultural factors driving the debates over reading methods in the United States since 1955.

Our project will also appeal to pre-service and in-service teachers who are tasked with delivering reading instruction in K-12 schools as well as teacher education program faculty responsible for preparing such teachers. Through historical narratives and author Bursuck's personal accounts, we provide practitioners and teacher educators with guidance that can help them make sense and give meaning to their own efforts helping teach children to read.

Finally, through our use of compelling real-world examples, memorable personal and professional experiences, and accessible language, our book will attract general readers who are interested in the historical context and current state of K-12 education. Many Americans recognize that reading is an essential skill for children, especially children who are at an early age. Our project helps illuminate why reading has achieved such strategic importance in our nation's educational reform rhetoric and policy actions, why the reading achievement gap has been so difficult to solve, and what strategies might guide future efforts at improvement.

In the end, we hope all readers gain insights into and even inspiration from America's seemingly unceasing yet unfulfilled quest to improve reading in our schools. We hope, in essence, that our book speaks to the teacher, the researcher, and the reformer of reading instruction inside of you. Finally, our thanks to Greg Conderman, Brooke Blanks and Gretchen Robinson for their supremely helpful feedback on drafts of our book.

Chapter 1

Introduction

This is a book about the struggles over reforming reading instruction and the corresponding effort to improve reading achievement in the United States over the last seven decades. The authors' interests in these subjects are both scholarly and personal. As researchers, the authors have each spent their academic careers studying the teaching of reading, instructional improvement, policy analysis, and educational reform. They have also had the opportunity to work as K-12 school practitioners (as well as alongside K-12 school practitioners) who were tasked with carrying out reading reform-related programs, projects, and strategies in schools. The authors' concerns in this book, then, range from national policies to the personal experiences of theirs and others connected to reading instruction and reform in the United States since 1955.

Given the nature of this project, the authors start by sharing a vignette related to their professional experiences with reading instruction and reform. First, author Bill Bursuck remembers:

It was the closing decade of the twentieth century. Reading education was emerging from a decade of instruction in which the conventional wisdom was that given a literature-rich environment, and a purpose for reading, children would learn to read as naturally as they learned to speak and understand oral language. It was the teacher's role to arrange the classroom environment in such a way that reading would develop naturally.

From his days as a rather unsuccessful beginning reading teacher in Buffalo, New York, to his years as a special education teacher and professor, Bill Bursuck had had a keen interest in finding effective ways to teach children at risk or with other special needs to read. Bill had become a strong advocate for a more systematic, explicit approach to reading instruction that included, but was by no means confined to, systematic, explicit phonics instruction.

Bill was encouraged by a series of research findings that the decision of which reading approach to use didn't have to be an either-or decision. The research was showing that as many as 30–35 percent of children learned to read quite naturally, while the remainder required instruction of varying degrees of care to become fluent readers. Bursuck was convinced that such a system of instruction could be delivered through what came to be known as multitier instruction and that phonics and other essential reading skills could be delivered systematically and explicitly based on need, not the philosophical orientation of the teacher. He felt that in this way the either-or, one-size-fits-all mentality of the reading wars could be avoided, a win-win, or at least that is what he thought would happen. Along with his colleague Shirley Dickson, Bill had developed and piloted a multitier model, which resulted in receiving a federal model demonstration grant, Project PRIDE. Bill implemented it in three low-performing, diverse, low–socioeconomic status (SES) schools in an urban Midwestern city school district.

Project PRIDE was the opportunity of a lifetime. Unlike earlier in his career, Bill felt he now had the knowledge he needed to truly make a difference, that his program would improve reading scores significantly and that PRIDE would be a beacon of hope and a model for the entire school district. The initial response of teachers to the model was mixed, but Bill and his project director Mary Damer were able to win over most of them by providing continuous, positive, support. This high level of assistance led to the program being carried out as designed and with positive results.

Project PRIDE had by no means eliminated the achievement gap in project schools, but the percentage of students meeting standards according to the state high-stakes assessment at each school did increase meaningfully, with one school more than doubling its rate from 31 percent to 67 percent. After the grant, Bill and Mary surveyed teachers as to whether they would want the project to continue. Around 29 or 85 percent of the teachers responded, and 28 or 97 percent of the teachers wanted the project to continue. One teacher commented that her students were able to read the trade books in her classroom for the first time—this was a teacher who was at first the project's biggest skeptic. While PRIDE hadn't made every child a reader, it had made a meaningful difference and established a foundation of reading instruction on which to build.

Bill always felt that if he could show results, the school district would recognize it and begin to use the multitier model in other district schools that had a high percentage of struggling readers. However, in May of the final year of the project, the district hired a new superintendent. At that time, thirty of fifty-two district schools were either on the State Department of Education's categories of "warning," "watch," or "corrective action." Nonetheless, instead of examining existing practices to see what might be working, and proceeding from there, the superintendent had his own ideas, and that involved "balanced literacy," not multitiered, direct instruction.

While Bill felt his model was already balanced, balance to the new superintendent meant less systematic, explicit instruction, particularly when it came to phonics instruction. When the principal at one of the PRIDE schools resisted, she was transferred, but not before she was accused of cheating on the state tests, a charge for which she was eventually cleared. The highest achieving school was also discouraged from continuing Project PRIDE, and their principal was eventually transferred as well. A recent Google of the 2016–2017 school report card results for the three project schools revealed reading proficiency rates far below those at the end of the project. The gains had evaporated.

Author Craig Peck has also experienced the personal impact of reading and school reform. For instance, he remembers:

During the 1990–1991 school year, Craig had completed his initial teaching assignment at an urban California high school as a member of the first cohort of Teach for America. Though it was originally intended that he would serve as an English teacher, Craig was instead reassigned a few days before classes began to teach five periods of world history. He taught in five different mobile home trailers converted to classrooms. Until he received a classroom set of textbooks in the midyear, Craig pushed around a cart with forty copies from classroom to classroom.

Craig cared about his students and learned very much from them. However, he was ill-equipped instructionally and, in retrospect, unequipped emotionally to thrive and persist as a ninth grade teacher in an urban high school. As a young white male who had just completed his degree at Harvard, Craig was simply unprepared to consider the stark realities that his students faced every day.

Craig still remembers some students, particularly those whose negative past learning experiences and general life circumstances complicated their pursuit of knowledge in his class. One mixed-race youth, for instance, wore clothing that suggested that he was an incipient gang member. However, he always began each day with a simple "Hello, Mr. Peck" and a smile. From what Mr. Peck could tell, he was unable to read and write beyond copying down notes Craig wrote on the chalkboard. He could not write any short answers on his own nor did Craig have the sense that he was getting any meaning from in-class readings.

To adapt to his needs and the needs of other students who struggled with reading, Craig checked out youth books about history from the local library. The books had pictures to help explain the text. He would use the Risograph machine on campus to copy these higher-interest, more accessible books for classes to use in their lessons.

The teaching adjustments Craig made related to students' reading abilities nonetheless left him with a dilemma: what could he really do as a ninth grade world history teacher to help students who were below or far below grade level in their reading? It was a dilemma that Craig was unable to resolve to his satisfaction or the genuine service of students during that year as a high school teacher. It is also a dilemma that still endures and confronts too many high school teachers today.

BACKGROUNDS, PURPOSE, AND SCOPE

As the preceding two vignettes suggest, the authors have been deeply involved with reading and school reform both professionally and personally. Bill Bursuck began his teaching career as an urban third and fourth grade teacher, worked as a special education teacher in Vermont, and upon receiving his Ph.D. in special education, had a thirty-year career in higher education preparing teachers and conducting research in reading and inclusive practices. After leaving his position as a high school teacher in 1991, Craig Peck embarked on a career journey that saw him teach in several urban school settings, obtain a Ph.D. in the history of education, and serve as a public high school principal in New York City. In 2007, he became a faculty member in the Department of Educational Leadership and Cultural Foundations at UNC Greensboro, which is where he met Bill who was concluding his career as a professor of special education.

Despite over fifty years of trying to solve it, the achievement gap in reading remains one of our country's most difficult problems. The purpose of this book is to help shed light on this problem by providing an accessible history of reading instruction and reform in the United States since 1955. While the search for the best way to teach reading is centuries old, reading instruction only became a major part of public policy debates and actions in the final two decades of the twentieth century. During and since that time, the field of reading has undergone multiple internal struggles that continue to influence the reading policy debates of today. Moreover, reading instruction became and remains a central element in major educational policy and reform initiatives meant to transform and fundamentally improve American education.

The scope of this book is threefold. First, the authors consider key developments over time in the field of reading instruction. The authors also examine important policies and reform trends that have occurred over the past six decades. Second, the book pairs the authors' accounts of two major historical periods of reading instruction and reform with the accounts of Bursuck's experiences as a professional whose forty-year career in education reflects a deep involvement in teaching, researching, and implementing reading methods. Finally, the authors connect public history with personal experience as they offer central lessons they learned through the study and practice of reading instruction and reform.

WORKING DEFINITION OF READING

For the purposes of this text, reading is defined as a multifaceted process through which a person comes to understand the written text. Reading text for meaning requires three basic abilities: identifying words in print or decoding; constructing meaning from the words recognized or comprehension; and coordinating word recognition and comprehension in such a way that the reading process is accurate and efficient, a skill often referred to as fluency. The authors also recognize the importance of developing and sustaining motivation to read, the absence of which can make all of the other component skills of no practical relevance.

"Language is a system of symbols that we use to communicate feelings, thoughts, desires and actions" (Friend & Bursuck, 2019, p. 216). Language can be oral (listening and speaking) or written (reading and written expression). While the authors realize that there is a reciprocal relationship among all forms of language and that it is current practice to combine reading and writing using the term "literacy," the clear focus of this book is on reading. The authors focus on reading because of its rich research and teaching history, its long-held prominence in the commercial arena via the ever-popular basal reader, and its current position as the object of continuous public policy efforts.

While most educators would likely agree on this general definition of reading, just how these parts are put into practice has been a matter of great disagreement, often, the authors believe, to the detriment of young learners. That position can best be understood by examining three common models or ways that the reading process has been traditionally explained: context, decoding, and automaticity (Kamil, 2015).

The context model, often referred to as meaning-based or top-down, emphasizes comprehension rather than decoding or efficient word reading, reflecting the idea that readers start with comprehension and work down to decoding *only when necessary*. The context model deemphasizes the importance of systematic, explicit decoding instruction, including phonics. This model is often referred to as *meaning-based* because of its emphasis on comprehension over decoding.

The decoding model, often referred to as the "code emphasis" or "bottom-up" model, emphasizes decoding as the first step in reading, whereby the reader learns to identify increasingly larger linguistic units as a *crucial first step* in making meaning out of the text (Ehri, 2020). In this model, decoding or word identification skills, largely though not exclusively phonetic in nature, are emphasized first.

The third model, automaticity, also emphasizes the initial need for decoding, but its emphasis is on the necessity of word identification skills being fluent or automatic in order for comprehension to occur. Like the decoding model, in the automaticity model, decoding takes a primary role early in reading instruction, with a particular emphasis on ensuring that it is fluent.

In this book, the authors take an approach called the *simple view of reading* (Gough & Tunmer, 1986). This approach recognizes that what to teach in beginning reading is not an either-or proposition. In this view, both decoding and reading comprehension are crucial skills to nurture in the beginning reader and both need to be taught carefully. Decoding is taught early, but so is comprehension in the form of oral language comprehension.

Oral language comprehension skills are an essential foundation for reading comprehension and act as a stand-in for reading comprehension until a learner's decoding skills are fluent. The idea is that once foundational language comprehension and decoding skills are in place, reading comprehension instruction can proceed with a greater likelihood of success. The authors prefer the simple view because it readily allows for the clear identification of the three major reading problems: decoding, language/reading comprehension, and a combination of the two.

The teaching of decoding skills usually includes *phonics*, which is the study of the relationship between letters and the sounds they represent. Phonics enables beginning readers to decode words by translating letters into sounds. Fluent decoding allows readers to recognize familiar words automatically and read new words independently. The teaching of phonics is in contrast to more naturalistic methods of teaching decoding, which stress figuring out words by looking at the first letter and then using the context to decide what makes sense. In this method, sounding out whole words is de-emphasized.

Phonemic awareness is an early language skill foundational for phonetics that is often taught alongside it. Words in the English language are made up of approximately forty-one to forty-four sounds called phonemes. Phonemic awareness is the ability to hear these smallest sounds in spoken language and manipulate them. Students who are at risk, have reading disabilities, or are English language learners are less likely to acquire phonemic awareness skills naturally; therefore, these skills need to be taught directly.

Our simple view of reading also emphasizes the importance of using systematic, explicit instruction to teach all reading skills, including phonics and phonemic awareness. Systematic, explicit instruction is of benefit to all students but is particularly helpful for students who fail to acquire beginning reading skills more naturally. *Explicit instruction* is the clear, direct teaching of reading skills and strategies that include the following:

- Clear instructional outcomes
- Clear purpose for learning
- Clear and understandable directions and explanations
- Adequate modeling/demonstration, guided practice, and independent practice
- Clear, consistent corrective feedback on student success and student errors (Bursuck & Damer, 2015, p. 14).

Systematic instruction is a teaching that clearly identifies a carefully selected and useful set of skills and then organizes those skills into a logical sequence of instruction (Bursuck & Damer, 2015). Sometimes the extent to which teaching is systematic and explicit is referred to as instructional intensity. Students vary along a continuum as to the degree of systematic, explicit instruction they need. Some children may learn to read quite naturally while others may require instruction that is much more intensive. It is a key idea of this book that the decision to teach systematic explicit phonics, or any reading skill, is not an either-or proposition. It depends on the student.

The simple view of reading stresses the importance of *both* systematic, explicit decoding and comprehension instruction, a position adopted by the authors of this book that Pearson (2012) has referred to as the "radical middle." The simple view does not suggest, however, that decoding and comprehension are of equal complexity. Of the two, comprehension is much more complex. The key point is that both skills are necessary and need to be carefully taught in order for more students to become accomplished readers.

A LASTING CRISIS IN READING ACHIEVEMENT

Reading has been described as the gateway to all other achievements as well as full participation in society. In the words of Castles, Rastle, and Nation (2018), "Reading transforms lives" (p. 5). Yet, despite its importance, millions of children in the United States are failing to learn to read. Certainly, reading is not an easy task. In the words of John Steinbeck:

> Some people there are, who, being grown, forget the horrible task of learning to read. It is perhaps the greatest single effort that the human undertakes, and he must do it as a child (Steinbeck, 1976).

According to the 2017 National Assessment of Educational Progress (NAEP), 35 percent of fourth graders and 35 percent of eighth graders were reading at levels considered proficient. Levels in urban districts were even lower, with 28 percent of fourth grade students reaching proficient levels (range = 5–42 percent) and 27 percent of eighth grade students (range = 7–36 percent). Results from the 2019 NAEP were even lower for all of these groups.

The failure to learn reading has consequences both for those who struggle to read and society as a whole. Struggling readers are more likely to drop out of school and less likely to leave school with the skills necessary to obtain fruitful employment. Struggling readers are also more likely to be in poor physical and mental health, misuse medication, commit crimes, and be dependent on government support, all at great cost to society (Castles et al, 2018). Experts estimate that over 90 million adults lack the literacy skills necessary in society, as a result losing over 200 million dollars in income a year (Whitehurst, 2003). To say that our society is in crisis mode concerning the reading achievement of its citizens is an understatement and begs the question as to why.

READING REFORM OVER TIME: A CONTENTIOUS PUBLIC POLICY HISTORY

The lasting crisis in reading achievement has led to persistent efforts to improve reading instruction. For half a century, the field of reading has been engaged in a continuous back-and-forth questioning of what is the best way to teach reading, particularly for learners who are at risk, have disabilities, or whose primary language is one other than English. To present our history of how reading has progressed over the last sixty years, we have divided our discussion into two parts.

The publication of *A Nation at Risk* in 1983 serves as the dividing line between one era that predated intensive, testing-focused school accountability and the succeeding era in which it was eventually incorporated throughout. Here, we provide a summary of the policy history that we will present in more depth in chapters 2 and 3.

Before 1983

As signified by policies and practices that emerged during this era, different goals informed and fueled the focus on reading reform. First, policymakers and public figures asserted that teaching reading to combat illiteracy would help students who are at risk due to poverty, racism, and other negative socioeconomic factors. Second, some writers like Malcolm X saw reading as essential for personal liberation, explaining how reading provided self and group empowerment for disenfranchised peoples.

Before 1955, reading instruction was dominated by instruction in word identification (as opposed to comprehension), and the predominant method was called "look-say," which involved mainly the memorization of whole or "sight" words. All of that changed with the publication of Rudolf Flesch's *Why Johnny Can't Read*. Flesch adopted a "take no prisoners" approach as he argued forcefully and persuasively for a phonics or sounding out approach in beginning reading.

Flesch's effort resulted in two research efforts whose purpose was to clarify which approach to teaching beginning reading was indeed better: Jean Chall's *Learning to Read: The Great Debate*, which reviewed the literature on effective beginning reading practices, and *The Beginning Reading Studies*, a federally funded series of studies designed by a group of reading researchers comparing all the major reading programs then in use. A third national study, Project Follow Through, addressed the issue but not as directly by comparing the effectiveness of four primary school models used as a follow-up to Head Start.

All three studies showed that systematic phonics was more effective than look-say in promoting word recognition and that the best results were obtained through a combination of systematic phonics and comprehension instruction. The results also showed that other teacher, school, and school district factors had an impact on reading outcomes.

Unfortunately, rather than building a consensus and future plan based upon both sets of findings, educators stressed the finding most closely aligned with their philosophy. Phonics advocates tended to focus on the phonics finding and more comprehension-based advocates, who comprised much of the reading establishment at the time, emphasized teacher, school, and district-related factors while de-emphasizing or even disparaging the role of phonics. Thus was the table set for several decades of reading wars.

The period 1955–1983 also witnessed the beginning of federal efforts to fight poverty, and at the heart of that effort was the hope of empowering young people with the gift of reading. Policymakers and public figures declared that teaching reading to fight illiteracy would help students confronted by poverty, racism, and other negative socioeconomic influences. Part of the effort to fight poverty through education involved a federal effort to target the reading and math achievement of children living in poverty. The Elementary and Secondary Education Act (ESEA) was passed in 1965 to attain that end.

The Great Society programs did mandate reading supports and eventually standardized tests for evaluating them. However, unlike the reading experts at the time, Title 1 framers had little interest in the matter of how best to teach reading. The perception at the time was that the achievement gap was due to a lack of money and resources, not a lack of expertise on the part of the schools.

The federal government had little interest in the nuts and bolts of education in the classroom, which was considered to be a matter left to states and local districts. In all, by 1982, millions of children were receiving supplemental help in reading. The results were considered a modest success, though the gap between rich and poor students remained.

This period also witnessed an increased federal role in special education as shown by the passage of the Education for All Handicapped Children Act of 1975, now called the Individuals with Disabilities Education Act (IDEA). One feature of the law particularly relevant for reading was the inclusion of learning disabilities (LD) within the federal categories of disabilities for the first time. LD was, and remains, the largest disability category and the category most difficult to accurately diagnose. That, combined with the fact that roughly 80 percent of students with LD have problems reading, in later decades led to problems of over-identification, which in turn directed public attention to problems with reading instruction in general education as a whole.

Research regarding teaching reading to students with disabilities was also beginning to inform approaches used in teaching reading to students of poverty in urban areas. For example, research was showing that both students with LD and students living in poverty tended to respond favorably to instruction that was systematic and explicit, a finding leading to continuing tensions between special and literacy educators.

While reading served different social purposes in the 1960s and 1970s, reading also served a bottom-line economic purpose of generating profits for publishers of reading texts and programs. Commercially produced readers could potentially bring about change efficiently and practically because everybody used them. However, commercial readers could also limit teachers' abilities to address specific learning situations or individual student needs. This tension was to play out more fully in the decades to come as reading reform assumed a more prominent position on the nation's education policy agenda.

After 1983

School reform as a major societal movement gained substantial momentum in 1983 with the publication of *A Nation at Risk*, which made education reform an economic issue. *A Nation at Risk* argued that the nation's economic woes at the time amounted to "committing an act of unthinking unilateral, education disarmament." The report resonated with the public and the connection between reading and the economic well-being of our country is a theme that continues to connect with the public at large today. As a result, education in general, and reading instruction in particular, were no longer back-burner issues left to local school districts to sort out. Education was now a front and center issue, setting the stage for a flurry of reading policy initiatives at the dawn of the twenty-first century.

Two key reading initiatives were undertaken during this period: whole language and accountability-based reading reform. Whole language had its origins in the 1960s as research in reading expanded to other fields such as sociology, psychology, linguistics, and psycholinguistics. The field of reading increasingly began to focus on cognition and comprehension as opposed to word identification (Pearson, 2000).

Whole language was promoted as a philosophy rather than a specific set of practices. According to whole language advocates, children weren't taught to read but learned to read naturally, much as they learned to speak, constructing meaning from written texts. Teachers assumed the role of facilitators, rather than dispensers of information. Whole language emphasized performing authentic reading tasks, not prepackaged basal reader lessons and practice-oriented worksheets. Phonics was considered unnecessary, and its use was actively discouraged.

There was also a political element to whole language that led to its popularity with teachers. Teachers loved the fact that with whole language instruction, ordinary teachers were considered the experts, leaving little room for prescribed basal reading programs or the groups of experts ordinarily involved in conducting professional development. As a result, the use of whole language spread so rapidly that by the late 1980s and early 1990s it was considered to be the "conventional wisdom" in reading instruction (Pearson, 2004).

In the end, however, whole language experienced a rapid fall from grace, starting in 1992 with California's fourth graders performing poorly on the NAEP compared to those from other highly populated states. While the poor performance in the reading of California's fourth graders was likely due to multiple reasons, ultimately, whole language was largely blamed. Its dogmatic sympathy for a nearly skills-free approach to reading instruction had alienated many educators, not just those favoring the use of phonics, but teachers who favored other types of skill instruction related to comprehension. Added to this was whole language's dismissal of the value of traditional reading assessments at a time when there was considerable public support for high-stakes, standardized testing (Pearson, 2004).

The 1980s and early 1990s had seen the rise to prominence of quantitative research as a driver of state and federal policy. Quantitative research involves investigating cause and effect relationships between teaching and learning using numerical data, often in the form of test scores. The Great Society programs had mandated the teaching of reading in general, as well as the use of standardized tests to evaluate reading instruction. However, since the *Coleman Report* in the 1960s, which stressed the impact of poverty over actual teaching, the public had seemed generally content with Title 1's compensatory model of funding students based on the number of low-income students in a school. In this approach, requiring the use of specific instructional strategies was off-limits.

The approach to reading reform began to change with the *Effective Schools Movement* (Edmonds, 1979). Edmonds and colleagues asked the simple question, "What are successful schools doing?" They used quantitative research methods to identify teaching practices used in high-achieving schools with the intention of preparing lower-achieving schools to do the same. The Effective Schools Movement promoted the idea that there was no excuse for not doing anything about the achievement gap between the rich and poor students. Edmonds's research paved the way for a greater demand for quantitative research methods over more traditional qualitative sources such as testimony from practitioners and evaluations of compelling cases. The methods Edmonds used to identify effective practices also went beyond the classroom to the school level.

The increasing emphasis on quantitative research in reading was also evident in the 1985 publication of *Becoming a Nation of Readers*, a synthesis of reading research conducted since Chall's landmark study in 1967. The study concluded that we already knew enough about reading to greatly improve reading instruction in the United States. This finding was echoed in another review conducted by Marilyn Adams, as reported in her influential book, *Beginning to Read: Thinking and Learning About Print*. Both *Becoming a Nation of Readers* and *Beginning to Read: Thinking and Learning About Print* recommended an approach to reading instruction that included well-designed phonics instruction along with support for oral language, reading comprehension, and written expression.

In 1998, The National Research Council issued a 390-page report synthesizing the quantitative research to date on effective ways to teach reading. Like *Becoming a Nation of Readers* and Chall's study before that, the report endorsed an approach to teaching beginning reading that included phonics in early reading instruction within a total reading program that also stressed oral and written language. Add to the National Research Council's findings the results of a series of studies conducted under the guidance of The National Institute of Child Health and Development (NICHD) showing that early intervention in the form of systematic, explicit phonics could reduce reading failure.

Some in the popular press heralded these research findings and declared an end to the reading wars. Nonetheless, politicians in several states were so disillusioned with the lack of phonics in the whole language approach that they weren't taking any chances. By 1999, thirty-six states had passed or had legislation pending promoting the use of phonics instruction including professional development for teachers on how to use it.

Congress, for its part, felt the need for another research synthesis, resulting in the *Report of the National Reading Panel* (*NRP*). *NRP*, published in 2000, was the most methodologically rigorous review of the reading literature to date. The *NRP* only included studies that were quantitative and met high methodological standards. Congress intended to solve the problem of how to teach reading once and for all. While more methodologically rigorous, the findings of the *NRP* largely mirrored the literature reviews that preceded it. The report did try to encourage practitioners to focus on all aspects of reading by identifying five key parts of reading instruction that needed to be carefully taught: phonemic awareness, phonics, fluency, vocabulary, and comprehension.

As occurred in reactions to past reports, the *NRP*'s glass was either half empty or half full depending on the readers' preexisting beliefs about reading instruction. Phonics advocates tended to emphasize its scientific rigor and its confirmation of the importance of systematic explicit phonics instruction, particularly early on. Many in the traditional literacy establishment decried its narrow scope, its exclusive use of quantitative research studies in the analysis, and vested panel interests. The panel was also accused of misrepresenting its findings in a widely distributed executive summary of the report.

This period of reading reform culminated in the passage of the largest federal reading initiative ever, Reading First, which passed as part of the No Child Left Behind Act of 2001. In it, politicians of both parties agreed that there was a reading problem that needed to be addressed nationally and that teachers using scientifically based reading instruction as recommended in the *NRP* was the solution.

Requirements for receiving Reading First's generous amounts of money were quite specific, matched to guidelines for teaching the five areas of reading instruction identified in the *NRP*. Reading First was a far cry from the early days of Title 1 when money was simply given to schools with the understanding that it would be used for disadvantaged children. However, with increased specificity comes increased scrutiny. The rigorous requirements of the act, while rightly recognizing the importance of research-based practices and carrying them out with fidelity, chose to overlook the fact that the research base was still incomplete. Gaps in the research base made carrying out the law difficult and left its highly prescriptive selection process vulnerable to criticism.

Ultimately, two developments led to its downfall. First, there was a perceived scandal. Several researchers involved in making funding decisions also were involved in the commercial publication of reading materials. While direct ties between these researchers and project adoptions were never established, the perception of a conflict of interest was enough to cast doubt about the value of the overall project.

Second, the Institute for Educational Sciences evaluated Reading First. While the act had improved outcomes in areas related to word identification, the "kiss of death" was that there were no improvements in reading comprehension. The combination of the conflict of interest scandal and limited results changed the politics involved. The coalition between Democrats and Republicans responsible for the passage of the reform in the first place had also eroded. It was now more politically beneficial for Congress to cut the program than continue it. Reading First lost its political base and was canceled in 2008 with little protest.

More than ten years have passed since the close of the NCLB/Reading First chapter of the reading wars. While the shooting has quieted some, peace hasn't exactly broken out. First, a "best of both" approach emerged in the form of "balanced literacy." However, the meaning of the term "balanced literacy" became muddled, leading some to call it "whole language in disguise," and others to advocate not using the term altogether. Presently, the "science of reading" (Seidenberg, 2014) has emerged as the major focus of the 'reading wars' (Gabriel, 2021).

GOAL

The authors hope that their book helps illuminate why reading has achieved such strategic importance in our nation's educational reform rhetoric and policy actions, why the reading achievement gap has been so difficult to solve, and what strategies might guide future efforts at improvement. The sad part of this story is that we have had enough knowledge at our disposal to make a reasonable attempt to solve the reading crisis for almost half a century.

The authors are both passionately committed to a pragmatic, middle position when it comes to reading reform. They believe that staking out extreme positions (in policy or practice) is counterproductive, and, historically, has impeded progress and perpetuated what is commonly referred to as the achievement gap. From their perspectives as long-time practitioners and researchers, battles over how to teach reading have only hurt the cause of reading instruction, especially for students most reliant on schools as the main setting for their learning.

In this book, the authors examine how educators and policymakers have time and again allowed ideology to trump reality, helping to perpetuate an achievement gap between rich and poor, disabled and non-disabled, English speaking and non-English speaking, African American and white, and along various other demographic dividing lines in the United States.

In the end, the goal of the authors is to motivate educators and policy-makers to see beyond decades of conflict in hopes of eventually reaching a consensus about how to deliver reading instruction that meets the needs of all learners. Their "radical middle" position (Pearson, 2012) takes into account the research-based positions on all sides in the reading war: reading as word recognition, reading for meaning, and reading for pleasure. The authors believe that only by addressing reading consensually, using the best available evidence, can the nation begin to reduce an achievement gap that up until now has been so resistant to change.

CHAPTER PREVIEWS

In chapter 2, the authors recount major events in the field of reading and public policy that occurred between 1955 and 1983. These events preceded the reading policies that were to emerge in the decades that followed. The authors then explore reform goals that resonated during this era only to grow in the decades to follow. In chapter 3, Bill Bursuck describes the outset of his career as an elementary school teacher in Buffalo, New York, and, later, as a special education consulting teacher in Vermont. Whether teaching in an urban context or supporting teachers in a series of rural schools, reading instruction was an essential aspect of his experience as was his desire to change and improve the schools in which he worked to better serve students.

Chapter 4 relates the reading and school reform that emerged during the years after 1983. This period began in earnest with the 1983 publication of *A Nation at Risk*, which served as a foundational spark for the rise in federal interest and involvement in reading policy and instructional reform. The authors discuss the unfolding of nationwide attention to student reading performance, including a widespread effort to improve reading achievement in low-performing schools. Also described is the meteoric rise and eventual fall of the whole language movement, as well as the federal Reading First initiative, an offspring of the No Child Left Behind Act of 2002 that provided significant grant funding for the implementation and study of "scientifically based" reading practices.

In chapter 5, Bursuck describes his experiences during 1983–2008, when he was a mid-career practitioner who becomes a graduate student and then a teacher educator. Bursuck describes his work preparing teachers to teach reading to problem learners, as well as developing and carrying out a prevention-based, multitier model of reading instruction in urban elementary schools in the Midwest and South.

Finally, in chapter 6 the authors summarize and review key findings and themes from the previous five chapters. Specifically, they consider how and why the motivating aims underlying reading reforms operated in concert and in conflict during what has become an enduring public struggle over reading methods and reform. They conclude their project by explaining several central lessons they have learned from their study and their career work toward improving reading and reforming education.

Chapter 2

Teaching Reading 1955–1983

Instructional Disputes, Federal Involvement, and the Roots of Reform

While the search for the best method of teaching reading is centuries old, reading instruction didn't become a major part of public policy until the final two decades of the twentieth century. Yet, over the years the field of reading has undergone multiple internal struggles that continue to influence the reading policy debates of today. Unfortunately, while arguments regarding the best way to teach reading continue, generation upon generation of children, especially those of color and/or living in poverty fail to acquire this most critical skill.

The purpose of this chapter is to relate instructional disputes and public policies that occurred between 1955 and 1983 that helped move reading instruction to the national stage where it remains to this day. These events were also signs of the conflicts over reading policies that were to come in the decades that followed. The authors also consider three motivating factors behind the rise of reading as a national concern. These factors represent the roots of the pursuit of improved reading instruction.

CONTESTED INSTRUCTIONAL APPROACHES, CONTESTED RESEARCH

The publication of Rudolf Flesch's *Why Johnny Can't Read* in 1955 changed the reading landscape quite dramatically. Flesch's book was on the best seller's list for thirty-three weeks and syndicated in "countless" newspapers. Flesch advocated passionately for a phonics approach to beginning reading over the whole word approach that had prevailed the fifty previous years. The contentious tone of Flesch's book, combined with the fact that it was widely read by parents active in their children's schools, pushed the issue of how best to teach beginning reading into the political realm, where it remains to this day. The difficulties involved in conducting educational research as well as the complexity of the reading process itself have provided ample cover for both sides of the phonics issue over the years, with the glass being half full or half empty depending on one's philosophical position. As a case in point, the same research Flesch cited as supporting a phonetic approach was used by the whole word advocates to defend their meaning-based practices (Chall, 1967).

Two independent research efforts were undertaken to help clarify the question of which approach was most effective for beginning reading, phonics, or whole word. One was Jeanne Chall's exhaustive critical review of existing reading research and practice, *Learning to Read-the Great Debate*. The other was The First Grade Studies, a comprehensive, multi-project, federally funded national research study. In this effort, a group of distinguished reading researchers compared all of the major beginning reading programs then in use. A third large national study, Project Follow Through, also addressed the issue, though less directly. Follow Through was part of Lyndon Johnson's Great Society programs and was initially designed as a platform for extending head start into the primary grades.

Due to budget constraints, Follow Through became an experiment comparing thirteen sponsored instructional models spanning three broad categories of teaching practices: basic skills, cognitive conceptual, and affective cognitive. The basic skills model focused on directly teaching fundamental skills in math, reading, spelling, and language. The cognitive conceptual models stressed the development of "learning to learn" and "problem-solving" skills. The affective cognitive category emphasized the development of self-concept and positive attitudes toward learning and, secondarily, on "learning to learn" skills.

Reading achievement was one of several measured academic and social outcomes. The basic skills models taught systematic phonics as their major word identification strategy. The affective cognitive and cognitive conceptual models employed variations of whole word approaches that stressed comprehension over decoding.

Despite major differences in design, all three of these research efforts reached the same two basic conclusions: (1) systematic phonics, either by itself or in combination with traditional look-say basal readers, is more effective than look-say alone in teaching word recognition, and at least as effective in fostering comprehension and (2) within each model there were examples of successful projects suggesting that teacher, school, and school district factors also accounted for differences in student reading performance. Reading experts tended to emphasize one conclusion or the other, depending on whether they held to a phonics or meaning-based preference.

Ironically, and sadly in view of the pendulum-producing reading war that was to occur over the decades, The First Grade and Follow Through studies showed that the best results were obtained using an approach that combined systematic phonics and comprehension. Despite this, phonics advocates tended to emphasize decoding because students who can't identify words fluently won't be able to understand what they read. While there is some merit to this argument, comprehension does involve more skills than reading words fluently, understanding oral language for one.

Advocates for a whole word, more meaning-based approach comprised much of the reading establishment. They emphasized the importance of other teacher and school factors such as teacher support, class size, and quality of reading materials, while either ignoring, criticizing, or de-emphasizing the role of phonics. This group of educators was likely to refer to the need for a balanced approach that included both phonics and meaning emphases. However, their idea of phonics tended to be more token attention than systematic and explicit. Thus, the critical question of exactly how the balance between phonics and meaning was to be attained was to remain unresolved and the table was set for decades of reading wars. The debate over how to teach reading became a fight at the extremes rather than a search for compromise in the middle (Kim, 2008).

Reading as a Federal Policy Priority

While reading experts were confronting the question of which method of beginning reading was most effective, significant changes affecting education were beginning to occur at the federal level. Before 1965, and consistent with the tenth amendment to the U.S. Constitution, education was primarily a state and local matter. Nonetheless, federal involvement in education was beginning to change. The launch of the satellite Sputnik by the Soviet Union in 1957, and the resulting fear of falling behind the Soviet Union in space, prompted the passage of the National Defense Education Act in 1958, which provided support for the development of science curriculum.

Then came Lyndon Johnson's "Great Society," and among its concerns, the underachievement of children living in poverty. In 1965, Congress passed the ESEA Act. Title 1 of the act targeted the reading and math achievement of children living in poverty. The perception at the time was that the achievement gap between rich and poor learners was due to the lack of money and resources, not the lack of expertise on the part of schools. This idea was reinforced in the following year with the publication of the *Coleman Report*, a government-sponsored study that placed the causes of underachievement on poverty. Blaming schools for the achievement gap was far in the future.

The federal government had little interest in managing how the Title 1 money was to be spent given that specific prescriptions for change would conflict with local and state control of the schools. Unlike the reading experts at the time, Title 1 framers had little interest in the issue of how best to teach reading. The only policy constraints in Title 1 were that the money be spent-pent on children living in poverty and that it supplement, not supplant, current local and state efforts to teach these children.

As a result of Title 1, by 1982 about 3.5 million children were receiving supplemental help in reading (Jennings, Deming, Jencks, Lopuch, & Schuler, 2015). The results were considered a modest success. The overall achievement gap between the rich and poor students remained, but Title 1 supports did manage to enable many students to make small, relative gains in the early grades. In the end, though, the Title 1 grants were too small to truly balance the playing field as originally intended. Sadly, the grants failed to eliminate the overall inequalities in funding as well as the distribution of experienced teachers in high-poverty schools.

Reading and Special Education

The 1970s also witnessed an increased federal role in special education, leading to decades of growth in that field. In 1975, the culmination of years of court cases involving the exclusion of children with disabilities from a public education resulted in the passage of PL 94-142, the Education for All Handicapped Children Act. The act, now called The Individuals with Disabilities Education Act or IDEA, guaranteed children with disabilities an individualized education in the most "normal" classroom placement that still meets their needs.

One implication of the law for this discussion about reading was the inclusion of LD within the categories of disability eligible for services. LD was not formally recognized as a disability until PL 94-142 at least in part because finding an underlying organic cause for it was difficult. The definition of LD in the federal law has not changed in the nearly fifty years the law has been in effect. It is based primarily on symptoms; namely, a language disorder resulting in a range of reading, writing, and math disabilities of varying intensity. According to the federal definition, these academic difficulties result from "disorders in underlying psychological processes," processes that were and remain difficult to measure.

The federal law also defined LD in terms of what it is *not*: a sensory, cognitive, or emotional disability or a learning problem due to cultural or economic disadvantage or poor instruction. However, proving the negative has been as difficult as proving the positive. As a result, developing an accurate and meaningful process for determining whether a child qualifies for LD services under the law has been difficult.

Given the vagueness of the federal definition of LD, researchers at the time were finding few if any differences between students that schools were identifying as having LD and other struggling readers. It seemed that anyone could be declared LD, or not, depending on the intent of the multidisciplinary team making the decision. In addition to undermining the credibility of the LD category, these difficulties in establishing eligibility were to cause problems of over-identification in later decades and call attention to the quality of reading instruction provided in general education as a whole.

Problems diagnosing LD were bypassed by those educators who served students using the principles of applied behavior analysis (ABA). From a behavioral perspective, the failure to learn to read was not a problem within the student, but a matter of teachers not correctly applying the principles of operant conditioning. To behaviorists, all children could and would learn to read if the correct combination of antecedents and consequences could be arranged. The behavioral emphasis on breaking academic skills into their parts placed it squarely into the phonics camp. The behaviorists saw the failure to learn to read not as an LD but as the result of poor instruction, or what was mockingly referred to at the time as "dyspedagogia."

The federal government also showed an interest in using effective reading instruction as a tool against poverty with research regarding teaching reading to students with disabilities informing approaches used in teaching reading to students of poverty in urban areas. In addition, a central animating hope of empowering young people with the gift of reading propelled instructional reform efforts for children with disabilities and from poverty.

ROOTS OF REFORM

As signified by policies and practices that emerged during this era, different goals informed and fueled the focus on reading reform. First, policymakers and public figures asserted that teaching reading to combat illiteracy would help students confronted by poverty, racism, and other negative socioeconomic factors. Second, some writers framed the act of reading as essential for personal liberation. For instance, high-profile social protest leaders like Malcolm X explained how reading afforded self and group empowerment for disenfranchised peoples. Third, reading-focused texts, curricula, and other learning materials remained a profitable enterprise in ways that ensured education-focused publishers, program vendors, and consultants benefited financially from the intensive focus on teaching reading.

Reading to Fight Illiteracy and Poverty

As American society progressed in the twentieth century, the standard for literacy increased to the extent that authors and advocates portrayed illiteracy as an apparent crisis in the United States. The term *functional literacy* came to the fore in the 1930s. It described the ability to read: (1) most of the everyday print matters, usually at the fourth or fifth grade level; and (2) common texts such as newspapers and manuals (Stedman & Kaestle, 1988, p. 113). The idea was that functionally literate adults apply these skills to gain secure employment. Estimates of the number of adult illiterates at the time ranged from as many as twenty to twenty-three million (Kozol, 1980).

Functional illiteracy had broad effects on the economic prospects and the overall well-being of both adults and the nation. Irwin Isenberg, in his editor's preface to his 1964 collection of texts and articles titled *The Drive Against Illiteracy*, explained, "There are more than 8 million so-called functional illiterates in the country. . . . The signs of undereducation [*sic*] are frequently a place on the welfare rolls, a home in the slums, and, perhaps, worst of all, the absence of any real hope for the future" (pp. 3–4). The articles in Isenberg's book with titles such as "Illiteracy: The Key to Poverty" and "Reading Unreadiness in the Underprivileged" helped establish illiteracy as a root cause of poverty.

The author of *A Guide to Teaching Reading* published in 1958 emphasized the critical importance of the illiteracy problem.

> Anyone who fails to reach the level of functional literacy is handicapped in carrying on the normal activities of daily life. . . . Many of today's occupations require a high level of education and consequently a high reading level. For these reasons acquisitions of the principal goal of schooling a cultured society. The state cannot afford to leave this training to parents because some parents would be indifferent and others might actually belittle such training. (Hildreth, 1958, p. 12)

The concern for the importance of literacy for each individual's life prospects carried over to the public realm. As Jimmy Carter, the new governor of Georgia in 1971, explained "Every adult illiterate, every school drop-out, every untrained retarded child, is an indictment of us all. Our state pays a terrible price for those failures" (Kozol, 1980, p. xiii). Through brief portraits of the experiences of illiterate adults, Kozol described "the feeling of entrapment which so often overwhelms the man or woman who reaches the age of twenty-one or twenty-two and cannot read or write" and engages "in a whole line of defensive strategies against discovery by others" (p. 8).

Such public expressions of concern regarding the connection between illiteracy and poverty helped ensure that reading instruction became a crucial part of reformer plans for social improvement. In the early 1960s in Chicago, for instance, "staff members of an elementary school in Chicago . . . developed a series of parent clinics" in which "parents are . . . urged to teach the children nursery rhymes and read them stories" (Reed 1964, pp. 154–55). In 1962 in Philadelphia, meanwhile, the school system attempted to address adult illiteracy through *Operation Alphabet*, a "TV literacy education series" that was intended to provide "the illiterate the opportunity to learn basic reading and writing skills in the privacy of his own home and through the already familiar medium of television" (Parker, 1964, pp. 152–53). As discussed previously, such local efforts at improving reading received national encouragement and funding through Title I of ESEA signed into law in 1965. By the mid-1960s, efforts were well underway to combat illiteracy by improving students' reading skills.

As the 1970s progressed, reformers focused explicit attention on improving reading instruction in schools. For instance, Dr. Kenneth B. Clark helped design a plan intended to start literacy among African American students in Washington, D.C., by holding educators directly accountable for reading the test results. Clark was a nationally prominent African American psychologist whose testimony was crucial in the *Brown v. Board of Education* decision. Unfortunately, intense real-world educational politics and an idea-stifling bureaucracy impeded their plans (Cuban, 1974). Other efforts to reform urban schools through teacher accountability in the 1970s met similar fates.

Despite failed efforts to reform schools generally and the teaching of reading specifically, the focus on results-oriented education led ultimately to the Effective Schools Movement, covered in chapter 4, in which the researchers identified and publicized best practices in high-performing urban schools. Independent efforts to improve reading access also emerged.

The Reading Is Fundamental organization, for instance, began in 1966 as one woman's effort to collect donated books and distribute them in Washington, D.C. This program eventually grew into a national organization concerned with improving reading access and ability, such as through a book offering tips that encouraged children's literacy. The rise and use of bookmobiles as roving book distribution centers extended further the idea that fostering a nation of literate adults was the key to enabling individual success and national prosperity.

Reading for Personal Liberation

While the importance of teaching reading to promote literacy and combat poverty marked one prevailing theme during the 1960s and 1970s, another theme held reading as a fundamental tool of social justice. This was particularly true of African Americans, a people who had long fought against injustice, racism, and oppression simply to pursue the ability to read. In learning to read, African Americans sought to master not only the technical ability to process information but to find deeper meaning in words, language, and symbols.

For instance, when the future Civil Rights leader Malcolm X entered prison in the 1940s to serve a sentence for robbery, he was functionally literate. However, he used his time behind bars to gain a thorough understanding of important philosophical and historical works in ways that broadened his perspectives and sharpened his debating skills. He noted in *The Autobiography of Malcolm X* that was published in 1964 at the height of the civil rights movement,

> I have often reflected upon the new vistas that reading opened to me. I knew right there in prison that reading had changed forever the course of my life. As I see it today, the ability to read awoke inside me some long dormant craving to be mentally alive. I certainly wasn't seeking any degree. . . . My homemade education gave me, with every additional book that I read, a little more sensitivity to the deafness, dumbness, and blindness that was afflicting the black race in America. . . . You will never catch me with a free fifteen minutes in which I'm not studying something I feel might be able to help the black man. (p.177)

Malcolm X's *Autobiography* suggested the degree to which reading could and did fuel personal liberation for an African American man.

Several years later in 1968, African American Civil Rights activist and one-time Black Panther Eldridge Cleaver described a similar awakening through reading in his series of letters from prison collected in the book *Soul on Ice*. In a letter from Folsom Prison in California, he explained, "I had evolved a crash program which I would immediately activate whenever I was placed in solitary: stock up on books and read, read, read; do calisthenics and forget about the rest of the world" (Cleaver, 1991, p. 54).

The idea of reading as a gateway to freedom was also reflected in the teachings of world-renowned and influential Brazilian scholar Paulo Freire, who conducted extensive work during the period that connected literacy and liberation. In the early 1970s, he wrote, "Acquiring literacy does not involve memorizing sentences, words or syllables—lifeless objects unconnected to an existential universe—but rather an attitude of creation and re-creation, a self-transformation producing a stance of intervention in one's context" (Freire, 2013, p. 45). For people of color throughout the United States, learning to read could and did offer liberation.

Children who experienced difficulty learning to read required a different form of liberation. By 1968, books such as Gladys Natchez's *Children with Reading Problems* described the conditions affecting students who struggled as readers as well as potential solutions for their difficulties. In the text, authors such as Jeanne Chall offered strategies for finding a proper fit between text and reading. In the same Natchez book, Carl Rogers emphasized the need to help students achieve "a freedom in which the individual chooses to fulfill himself by playing a responsible and voluntary part in bringing about the destined events of the world he lives in" (Rogers, 1968, p. 428).

Testimony to the fruits of such freedom, Carol Moseley Braun attended school in the 1960s and overcame dyslexia to become the first African American United States Senator in the mid-1990s. Braun explained, "I see connections other people don't. I can see around corners. . . . We need to encourage these kids to believe in themselves, because if they are taught to, they will. And it is the kids who are, ultimately, the ones who are going to have to make their way" (Wallace, n.d.).

Reading Instruction as a Commercial Enterprise

While reading served different social purposes in the 1960s and 1970s, reading also served a bottom-line economic purpose of producing profits for publishers of reading texts and programs. Commercially produced readers, at least potentially, could bring about change more efficiently and practically because everybody used them. At the same time, dependence on what were essentially standardized products could potentially limit their ability to address specific learning settings or individual student needs. In her 1967 book, Jeanne Chall considered the possible negative effects of a situation in which a clearly identified problem met widely advertised solutions. She noted,

> In my visits to schools I found evidence over and over again that the companies that publish beginning reading materials play an important role in determining how children are taught to read. The representatives (salesman) of these companies are very able and persuasive, and many school administrators listen to them carefully. One administrator told me, "The publishers representatives are often more informed than the principals and teachers, who don't have time to be informed." Another specifically noted that it was the representative of a publisher, calling with a new program, who convinced the people in his school what reading program to adopt. (p. 297)

Once a school or district purchased a reading publisher's product, Chall explained, the relationship could continue through the vendor's provision of professional development services and supplementary supporting materials. In addition, vendors protected their products' reputations by citing "scientific evidence" in ways that promoted their products and challenged competitors' claims.

Though Chall assigned blame for the apparent profiteering to representatives from the publishing industry, she did also emphasize, "they are speaking to people [educators] who for the most part do not use objective research evidence as a criterion for selection" (p. 300). Thus, she concluded, "if they never look at the evidence, the job of overselling them cannot have been too difficult" (p. 300).

Supporting these points, Shannon (1988) noted, "since 1920 reading experts and commercial publishers have exerted more power than school personnel in and the public during the negotiations of what is to be considered the proper definition of reading and the appropriate way to teach reading" (p. 43). Clearly to some, the control of textbooks was a legitimate concern during this period, a theme that was to come to full fruition in the whole language era of the 1980s and 1990s.

However, others, particularly those who designed materials for students who required a more technical approach to instruction, saw commercial reading programs differently. They viewed these programs as effective platforms for providing the efficient, careful, high-quality instruction students at risk needed to catch up with their classmates. For example, the Direct Instruction programs used highly detailed scripts to ensure their meticulously designed programs were carried out accurately.

Other commercial programs such as those developed by Lindamood-Bell were not as heavily scripted but provided extensive, explicit support for teachers using them. It is noteworthy that programs such as these tended to include systematic, explicit phonics as a key part of the curriculum. Advocates for freeing teachers from basal were more likely to employ less-structured, meaning-based reading instruction.

Educators such as Anita Archer recommended preparing teachers and administrators to more effectively evaluate and, if needed, modify their commercial reading materials. For example, Archer designed an instrument to enable teachers and administrators to evaluate their reading materials concerning their effectiveness data and whether the instruction was systematic and explicit. These and other issues revolving around school use of commercially produced reading materials were to continue, all the way to the present.

CONCLUSION

As the 1960s and 1970s progressed, reading experts had yet to reach a meaningful agreement on how best to design beginning reading instruction. This state of affairs caused Flesch to once again rail against the reading establishment, this time in an updated version of his original book titled, *Why Johnny Still Can't Read: A New Look at the Scandal of our Schools*. There were also complaints that teachers in the 1970s were responding to the demand for more phonics with inappropriately designed "phonics drills, fill-in-the-blanks and circle-the-word workbooks and basal readers with text chosen more to instruct than inspire" (Esch, 1999, p. 1).

Jeanne Chall in "The Great Debate" had worried aloud about what would happen if a new wave of phonics instruction were to be implemented inappropriately:

> We will be confronted in ten or twenty years with another best seller: "Why Robert Can't Read." The culprit in this angry book will be the prevailing linguistic, systematic phonics or modified alphabet approach—whichever teaches whole words and emphasizes reading for meaning and appreciation at the very beginning. (p. 308)

Meanwhile, there were tensions at play in the roots of reading reform. On the one hand, reading for personal liberation and reading to fight illiteracy and poverty both suggested how the pursuit of individual change and social improvement were essential motivators in efforts to reform instruction. At the same time, reading instruction served as a profitable enterprise for companies and consultants, which ran the risk of working toward materialistic rather than nobler ends. In this way, we see the possible tension between reform for social justice and reform for financial returns.

In the late 1960s, even as Chall's book gained national recognition, events proved important in a personal way: Bill Bursuck entered the field of teaching for the first time. In doing so, Bill learned early on that issues related to reading and reform were linked to his success as an urban elementary school teacher. In chapter 3, Bill tells his story as an educator from 1968 to 1978 and describes how the policies and themes we have discussed here in chapter 2 relate to his own experiences.

Chapter 3

Experiences

Teaching Reading in Urban and Rural Settings, 1968–1978

Bill's first teaching experience was at an urban elementary school in Buffalo, New York. He then served as a consulting teacher in special education in rural Vermont. Each of these positions had its own set of challenges, challenges that were to be present throughout his almost fifty-year career in education.

BASIC TRAINING

In the spring of 1968, the last thing on Bill's mind was education, including his own. He was due to graduate from college and his mother, worried about his future from various angles, sent him information about the Teacher Corps program at Buffalo State College, one of many Great Society programs at the time designed to fight the "war on poverty." Bill had never taken an education course, but fortunately, that worked in his favor because the program preferred liberal arts majors much like the Teach for America program does today.

Bill's class of fellow Teacher Corps interns was far from diverse, consisting mainly of white, middle class, left-leaning types; out of a group of about thirty interns, two were black and one Hispanic. The Teacher Corps training was primarily field-based, a practice advocated by most teacher education reformers today.

Bill was part of a small team of interns working under the tutelage of a team leader, a "master teacher," at PS #6, an urban Buffalo elementary school. Bill's team leader, Frank, had been a highly respected teacher before his selection as a Teacher Corps team leader. Ironically, he was taken out of the classroom to be a team leader and the Teacher Corps interns rarely got to see him teach. Better if they could have all been a part of his classroom and been true interns, a reform in teacher education often recommended today. It was no surprise to anyone when Frank left the Teacher Corps after one year; he missed teaching the kids.

The students at School 6 were almost entirely African American and lived in the Talbert Mall, a racially segregated, high poverty, high-rise housing project constructed in the 1950s. The late 1960s was the era of urban black riots and Buffalo was no exception. The Buffalo riots took place in 1967, a year before Bill entered the Teacher Corps.

Like today, there was a significant gap in reading achievement between African American students and their white counterparts. However, as discussed in chapters 1 and 2, solving the achievement gap was commonly perceived as simply a matter of allocating more resources to urban schools. As a Title 1 school, Bill's school was inundated with federal programs. However, he would soon learn that making a difference in reading achievement in an urban area would take much more than that.

A key goal of designers of the Teacher Corps program was to better connect the higher education component with the demands of teaching in an urban environment. This was a novel idea at the time, and, disappointingly, still an issue today. The program started non-traditionally enough. Before the first school year, all interns were required to participate in a two-week orientation at the Buffalo State retreat in the rural Western New York town of Franklinville. Included in the experience was "sensitivity training," the purpose of which was to sensitize the interns to the needs of Buffalo's inner-city communities, and hence its students.

Good intentions aside, the idea of sensitizing mainly white middle-class graduate students to the realities of low-income areas while gathered in a pristine rural setting seems a bit ridiculous. One particularly memorable moment involved an intense discussion about whether locking one's car in an urban area would be perceived by the community as a violation of community trust. While the program recognized the cultural divide between urban schools and the community, exactly how this experience was to enhance interns' ability to teach reading or any other subject was not evident.

The master's degree component of the Teacher Corps experience was quite traditional. Although the degree Bill earned was listed on his transcript as Urban Education, except for an introductory sociology class on urban black culture, there was little evidence of course content directly related to teaching reading in urbanf settings. The results of the *First Grade Studies* and Chall's review of the literature were not included in the reading coursework, or at least not in a way that was coordinated with the interns' field sites. Of course,

Bill's total lack of background knowledge and experience at the time could have caused him to gloss over such content.

Reading instruction in field sites consisted primarily of basal readers similar to the ones discredited in the First Grade Reading studies except for having urban settings and multiracial characters, along with some unsystematic phonics sprinkled in, the likely result of Chall's advocacy for phonics in the 1960s. Neither setting resulted in Bill internalizing a coherent scope and sequence of reading skills, including phonics, that could have provided a blueprint for his teaching. Bill essentially taught reading by conscientiously following the basal reader and then making games to reinforce isolated reading skills.

The conventional wisdom was that students would learn to read if properly motivated. If Rudy can't read, find something to read in which he is interested. If a student lacks one isolated skill or another, construct a learning game to teach her to perform it. In Bill's later years as a teacher educator, he would refer to his reading methods classes during that time as Games 101, Games 102, Advanced Gaming, and so on. Truth be told, this was not the "game plan" needed, and the lack of student outcomes that resulted didn't seem to change the dynamic much. On Bill's final exam in reading methods, one of his last master's classes, he wrote only the following: "I'm tired of talking about teaching reading. I just want to do it." Bill's attitude, in retrospect, even at his own admission self-serving and immature, was also somewhat ironic, since at the time he had no concrete idea of how to teach reading.

Bill's first actual reading lesson came during year 1 of the Teacher Corps. At the time, he was living at home. Bill's mother was an English teacher turned reading teacher, but Bill couldn't recall having conversations with her about the teaching of reading per se. Most of her comments at home about her job involved her principal's lack of support for her reading program in general, not the nuts and bolts of how to teach reading. His mother taught in a junior high school setting and then, as now, the teaching of reading was not a priority among junior and senior high school staff and administration.

Unable to find anything specific enough about lesson plans and the basics of the teaching of reading in his college class notes, Bill was starting from scratch. Basal readers are often criticized because they are profitable, and can be based on commercial trends rather than hard research. Still, echoing Chall, basals are often *the* major source of information for teachers on how to teach reading.

For Bill, a starting teacher without a reading game plan, the basal reader teacher's manual was his bible, and like the real Bible, teaching from it was a matter of faith. He scripted out his entire lesson while sitting at the kitchen table. Bill was never one to wing it, at any level of teaching. The next day, following this reading lesson, Frank handed him a piece of paper that said something on the order of Bill Bursuck, Ph.D. in reading. Prescient perhaps, and at the time encouraging, but, while Bill didn't realize it at the time, it meant that even his master teacher hadn't internalized a systematic plan for how to teach reading.

Bill emerged from his first year in the Teacher Corps with two important understandings. The first was that if a child wasn't learning to read, analyze carefully what you are doing and change it, as opposed to blaming the child or his/her environment. This idea was somewhat unique for its time; like the thrust of the *Coleman Report*, schools tended to attribute the lack of student progress to the harmful effects of poverty.

From that time on, except for occasional bouts of frustration expressed mainly to his wife, Bill generally stayed away from infamous teacher lounge discussions about difficult students. To this day, he still believes in teacher responsibility, though the current trend to blame teachers alone for the achievement gap has caused him to temper his position somewhat. While Bill remains an advocate for teacher accountability, like education historian Diane Ravitch, he also believes that problems related to the effects of poverty on learning to read simply cannot be ignored. Still, Bill believes that poverty should inform teaching, not be an excuse to avoid it.

The second lesson from that first year involved classroom management, but not in the most common sense. Classroom management in urban schools could be a struggle, so much so, those initial efforts in this realm were commonly referred to as "baptism by fire." It became quite clear right away that you couldn't teach reading if your students weren't listening. Unfortunately, then as now, the rudiments of effective classroom management weren't normally a part of teacher education programs.

What the interns learned from Frank went beyond the basics of classroom management. While he didn't have his own classroom, the interns were able to observe Frank interacting with students one-to-one or in small-group settings. Frank treated each and every student with respect, as if he or she were the most important person in the world. Frank was able to connect on a strong personal level with his students. Bill can still remember the smiles he put on their faces; they felt truly loved. While the mechanics of classroom management need to be mastered by every teacher, effective teachers like Frank take it to the next level, and connecting with one's students is a critical part of teaching children to read.

THE WILL TO SURVIVE

Following the Teacher Corps, Bill took a position as a full-time fourth grade teacher at the school where he interned in the Teacher Corps. Despite considerable experience with classroom management in the Teacher Corps, establishing and maintaining classroom control remained an everyday concern. In other words, "baptism by fire" was more like purgatory, an extended experience. Bill remembers thinking that teaching would be indispensable training for being a judge, as the children demanded an absolute level of consistency that could be difficult to deliver.

Added to behavior problems were the many academic problems of his students. Bill's first class had only one or two students in the entire class reading at grade level. He remembers likening teaching in an urban school to coming into a town after a hurricane had just hit and trying to figure out where to start the clean-up. It was that daunting, and, as already explained, his repertoire of strategies to teach reading consisted mainly of the classroom basal and supplemental activities that were primarily motivational in nature.

In Bill's classroom, survival was the order of the day. Mercifully for Bill, though in retrospect sadly, tenure appointments were granted based mainly on classroom control and not on student achievement. Most of his class was below grade level in reading and math and remained so throughout their time with him. However, this was not for lack of trying. It's fair to say that Bill was perceived and respected as a good teacher, though, at this point in his career, he was more conscientious than competent.

Bill organized his students into three reading groups to ensure that instruction was at their appropriate reading levels. Reading groups were that era's version of differentiated instruction which then, as now, was a worthwhile, yet challenging concept to put into practice. The reality of having three reading groups was that students had to be working independently for two-thirds of the reading period. It also didn't help that Bill was teaching in a late nineteenth-century built classroom that had high ceilings, creating an echo effect that amplified the slightest sound.

Bill struggled to plan independent activities that were both educationally appropriate and kept the students quiet for extended periods. This proved difficult given students' deficient skill levels and much of the independent work devolved into worksheets and games of questionable value. Many articles over the years have been written criticizing instructional tracking, and much of the criticism is justified. Still, the task of differentiating instruction requires great skill and carefully designed professional development that many teachers never receive. Up to that point in his career, Bill certainly hadn't received any.

Bill supplemented his classroom reading program with an approach popular at the time called 'language experience'. The idea behind language experience was that students could be motivated to read and comprehend by using written samples of their own oral language as reading material. Language experience was one of the methods of reading instruction evaluated in the First Grade Reading studies and it tended to favor learners with a high degree of reading readiness skills, not the types of students who inhabited Bill's classroom. Besides, Bill's first class consisted of fourth graders, not first graders.

Language experience was an attractive option because most of Bill's students were reading at the first grade level, and this approach provided text that was relevant to the students' background and that they could readily memorize. Having students publish their own books was quite popular at the time and Bill took the stories his students had dictated and turned them into books. Students spent class time illustrating the books, an activity of questionable value that filled time so he could conduct his reading groups in peace. Students memorized their books and Bill sent them to other classrooms to read them to younger students. Students were so proud of themselves, and Bill was proud of them. It was professionally satisfying to engage them in a reading activity that Bill believed also enhanced their self-image.

A healthy self-image was an important educational goal then, as it was widely believed that a good self-image preceded reading competence, rather than being the result of it. It never occurred to Bill that by encouraging his students to read their books predominantly by guessing at words using contextual and picture cues, he was likely undermining their acquisition of the accurate, fluent word identification skills necessary for comprehension. Bill's heart was in the right place. Building his students' self-esteem by having them read to younger children was a sound and important teaching strategy. He just needed to better embed it within an overall systematic plan to teach his students to read.

Every month, Bill would drive to the downtown public library to borrow several boxes of children's books to take to class. Students would read them during their independent work time. Then, as today, reading independently was the gold standard for reading instruction. Unfortunately, what Bill failed to realize at the time was that silent reading needed to be carefully structured for it to be most effective. Children who haven't been reading consistently at home may not have a good idea of what to do with a book, including, most importantly, selecting books that they can read.

Bill did love reading the library books to his students. It was one of the most enjoyable teaching activities of the day for him, partly because he enjoyed the books and partly because the students were almost always attentive during this time. In retrospect, however, Bill felt he failed to take full advantage of the student's interest. He used a generally passive reading format, reading students a book while they listened passively. In this way, he missed valuable opportunities to engage them in discussions of vocabulary, character development, and plot—skills critical for reading comprehension.

Bill's use of children's literature is a good example of using a teaching approach based on whether the students enjoy it and not according to whether it taught them anything. Most disturbing perhaps is that he could have easily done both if he had been prepared to do so.

Looking back at Bill's first two years of teaching reading, one is struck by the idea that when it comes to effective reading instruction, details matter. Louisa Moats (2020) has famously referred to this as "reading as rocket science." On the surface, all of the reading activities just described would appear appropriate. Bill was individualizing instruction by grouping for reading, building self-image by publishing books the students wrote themselves, providing time for independent reading, and reading to his students every day.

Yet, Bill's instruction lacked a comprehensive scope and sequence of skills to guide it. In essence, he was unknowingly undermining his effectiveness as a reading teacher. Details such as what skills to teach, in what order, and how to structure silent reading are not glamorous; nor are they likely to be seen as particularly creative. Yet they can make a significant difference in student achievement.

During Bill's first two years of full-time teaching, he received little, if any, professional development. He did spend countless hours planning lessons with a colleague, a former Teacher Corps intern, and a friend who taught in the next door classroom. Bill and his colleague Bob were pretty much on their own, accountable only to themselves, and without the teaching tools to make a difference. Their classrooms were generally orderly, they submitted their lesson plans on time, and communicated frequently with parents through letters home, phone calls and even home visits. In short, they approached their jobs with a sense of enthusiasm and passion befitting young, idealistic, beginning teachers. Bill and Bob were seen by the administration as doing a great job. In fact, Bill's principal went so far as to personally appear before his draft board in support of his request for a teaching deferment.

Bill and his colleague benefited from a system that evaluated teachers strictly based on inputs. Teacher accountability was a thing of the future. In these days of hyper accountability, and with it varying degrees of push back, it's important not to lose sight of the fact that the reason for school reform in the first place was that the old system of no accountability wasn't working.

It is worrisome that the current backlash against testing, some of which is justified, may cause us to go back to a system of little accountability, which, as the early teaching experiences described here show, was not of benefit to students either. Bill and Bob were confronted daily with their students' serious reading difficulties, for which they had no systematic game plan. Added to that was the strain of managing difficult behavior day in and day out. These conditions made for a stressful experience.

Much of Bill and Bob's stress was self-imposed. They were young and idealistic and wanted things to change right away. Despite an achievement gap as wide as today's, there was a general lack of urgency when it came to getting students on grade level. During Bill's first fall as a full-time teacher, a colleague peered into his classroom on a Friday afternoon and expressed surprise that he was actually teaching.

The role of teachers' unions was also increasing. It seemed that every Labor Day it was unclear whether teachers were to report to their schools or the picket line. Many Fridays the school secretary, with a tone of surprise in her voice, would call Bill over the intercom to remind him to pick up his paycheck as he was usually the last person to do so. Teaching was more than a job for Bill, and, evidently, the secretary found that surprising. Ironically, all of this dysfunction was occurring at a time when multiple federal programs were being instituted in Bill's school as part of Title 1.

PROJECT FOLLOW THROUGH

In Bill's third year, he became a Follow Through third grade teacher. As described in chapter 1, Follow Through was a large federal experiment designed to compare three broad categories of interventions: basic skills, cognitive conceptual, and affective cognitive. At the time, Bill was largely unaware of any of this. All he knew was that after four years of teaching in urban schools—two in the Teacher Corps and two as a fourth grade teacher—he was still searching for a more effective way to teach his students to read.

A good friend whom Bill respected greatly as a teacher was teaching in the grade 1 Follow Through class at his school. Bill knew from her that Follow Through had more professional development opportunities and that as a Follow Through teacher he would have a full-time paraprofessional to assist him. Bill applied for an opening at his school and thus began his third year of full-time teaching as a third grade Follow Through teacher.

The Buffalo Follow Through program was sponsored by the Far West Laboratory, whose Responsive Education model, one of the affective cognitive Follow Through models, emphasized self-paced, self-determined instruction. The model was based on the assumption that given self-esteem and a learning environment organized according to the students' interests, academic learning would naturally follow.

The expectation was that the teacher would set up interest areas in all academic areas, much like learning centers used in today's classrooms. The students would circulate through the centers, guiding their own learning, with the teacher acting mainly as a facilitator. Responsive education was a variation of the open classroom environments that were popular at this time.

Bill's entering third grade students had gone through multiple teachers the previous year and they began the year acting as if they didn't expect him to last very long either. Ironically, the Responsive Model offered few clues as to how to be responsive to these particular students. Bill learned right away that his students lacked the background knowledge, reading skills, and sense of self-efficacy required to learn independently, despite having already spent first and second grades in the program. The entire class was reading below the grade level, with most of the students reading at the first grade level and below.

The primary method of teaching reading was the language experience approach that Bill had used previously with little success. Concerned about his students' lack of basic word reading skills, Bill incorporated some large-group phonics instruction into his morning reading teaching. He remembers someone associated with the program saying with a bit of disbelief something like, "he wouldn't be doing it if they didn't need it." Bill's use of large-group phonics did cause a bit of a stir in the program but no one told him not to do it.

Unfortunately, Bill lacked the expertise to extend this instruction much beyond teaching his students isolated letter sounds and guessing at words by using the first sound and context clues, a commonly used approach to early decoding that he learned from using the basal. Add to that, Bill's paraprofessional seemed to identify more with the students than him, talking and fooling with some of the students while Bill was teaching. What had promised to be a way forward as a teacher, turned into another turn at teacher survival.

Still, the support available through the program did relieve the sense of isolation that Bill had experienced the previous two years. Bill remembers one observation, in particular, conducted by Pat, the head of the program. During his post-observation conference, he apologized for the appearance of his classroom, noting the absence of fancy bulletin boards. In her response, Pat referred to one particular interaction Bill had with a student during the observation and said that the positive, affirming manner in which he had interacted with him was much more important than having fancy bulletin boards.

Follow Through, whatever its shortcomings, provided Bill with support for his teaching, a positive mindset toward teaching children in an urban area and a sense of professional community. These features of the program are reflected in this poem Bill wrote for the Follow Through Newsletter regarding the program's regular Saturday A.M. professional development sessions.

The November Grays—Look Out
Do you know what I'm talking about?
Ideas running thin—kids running fast
Is it me or them—is that what you ask?
Then comes Saturday—It's inservice again
Most agree with the why, if not with the when
For here we can grow—and at our own rate

Like we do with the kids—the consistency's great
Now don't get me wrong—at times they're unreal
And some of the speakers don't know how we feel
But there's much to be gained—more often than not
And on Monday school's better—So, thanks a lot.

FINDING BEHAVIORISM IN THE GREEN MOUNTAIN STATE

Whatever its merits, it was clear to Bill, and validated years later in the results of the federal *Follow Through* experiment, that meaningful student reading outcomes remained elusive. One weekend on a visit to his sister's house, Bill noticed an announcement in the educational job listings of the Sunday *New York Times* for a master's degree program in special education at the University of Vermont. The program stressed providing support for general educators working with students with special needs. The idea of moving to the country appealed to city boy Bill, but so did the possibility of learning to better teach struggling readers. Reflecting on his experience teaching in Buffalo four years later in his application letter for admission to doctoral programs, Bill summed up his perceptions this way:

> My education career began 10 years ago as an inner-city teacher in Buffalo, New York. It was there I learned that providing a steady stream of "creative, relevant" activities was not enough. Many of the children did not progress in spite of all my efforts. I left Buffalo for Vermont hopeful, but uncertain whether schools could control the variables critical to teaching children with learning problems.

Upon leaving for Vermont, a colleague who taught across the hall from Bill, a former Teacher Corps intern, congratulated him on his new position and told him that if he thought teaching children was difficult, wait till he tried to change teacher behavior! While ultimately she of course proved to be correct, still, beginning the Vermont Consulting Teacher (CT) program was nothing short of a revelation for Bill, starting with the fact that its offices were housed in a small house on campus that had unisex bathrooms. This program was definitely ahead of its time. Bill felt enough at home that he would often refer to the tree-covered Green Mountains as his "living room" mountains.

The CT program was a special education, training-based model of serving students with disabilities. Except for Burlington and three smaller cities, Vermont was a rural state. When the push to serve all students with disabilities (then called handicapped students) came, historically, most Vermont schools had been too small to serve these students in special schools or classes. Many students with disabilities remained unidentified and were taught in general education classes by teachers not prepared to teach them.

The idea behind the CT program was that, with the appropriate support, general education teachers could effectively serve most students with what would much later be called high-incidence disabilities (mild intellectual, learning, and emotional disabilities). Implicit in this was the idea that the same strategies that are effective for students with disabilities would also be effective for other hard-to-teach students in general education classes such as children living in poverty, "slow learners," and children for whom English isn't their primary language. CTs, graduates of the master's program at the University of Vermont, would carry out this training directly in the schools.

The technology driving the CT program was the educational application of the principles of applied behavior analysis (ABA). The director and creator of the program had received his doctoral degree from the University of Kansas, which was at the time a mecca for applied behavioral applications to educational settings. The key assumptions of the CT program were later best described by two of Bill's professors there as follows:

> All students can learn, regardless of their handicaps.
> All teachers can also learn, and therefore can learn to effect behavioral change in their learners.
> To evaluate teacher effectiveness, there must be behavioral change of the learners as a function of the programs the teacher implements.
> The most promising methods that seem to help teachers effectively change the educational and social progress of students are derived from the experimental analysis of behavior.

After Bill's less than satisfying experience teaching in Buffalo, he enjoyed basking in the warm, optimistic glow of positive thinking. In the Teacher Corps, Bill was taught that if a child wasn't learning to read, examine your teaching for answers and don't blame the students and their background. While this general message was correct, Bill felt he was offered few to no specifics for exactly how to accomplish it. Not only were these ABA folks pro-students, but they also had concrete guidelines for what to do. Problem-solving was simply a matter of figuring out how to apply the behavioral principles to a given situation. Bill had merely answered an ad in the *New York Times* and literally stumbled onto exactly what he had been looking for.

Bill took to behaviorism naturally and passionately. Gone was the shadow of the *Coleman Report* and the murky waters of the Teacher Corps. Bill had never encountered educators who were so sure of themselves, and in the beginning, that was refreshing and reassuring. He dove into behaviorism heart and soul and became a real convert to the cause. It didn't hurt that Bill's first year was spent in the comfortable bubble of the University of Vermont, far from the realities that would face him in year two, an internship experience in a Vermont school district.

The general instructional platform articulated in the CT program was DABIME—the data-based, individualized model of education. DABIME began with observing and measuring the academic or social behavior in question such as letter sounds or words correctly identified. The next step was to set an instructional objective specifying the outcome desired including the behavior in question, the conditions under which it was to be performed, and the criterion for judging whether the outcome had occurred.

As said previously, after years of having few to no strategies for solving the problems of struggling readers, Bill found DABIME quite attractive. Besides, there's a lot to be said for the ability to make a complex problem more manageable by reducing it in complexity. Feeling as if you are in control and that positive outcomes are likely can often lead to positive effects beyond the initial behavior(s) targeted for change. Once when working with the teacher and parents of a hyperactive kindergartener, a simple behavior change program begun at school to enable the child to remain in class interest centers for longer periods motivated his parents to improve his behavior during playtime using a similar program at home.

As for how DABIME applied to reading instruction, it is fair to say that it was a good example of the high level of pedagogical cockiness present in the behavioral community at this time. With ABA, the failure to learn to read was not viewed as a problem within the student, such as a learning disability, but as a matter of teachers not correctly applying the principles of operant conditioning. To behaviorists, all children could and would learn to read if the correct combination of antecedents and consequences could be arranged. Implicit in the behavioral mindset at the time was the idea that if general education teachers could be appropriately prepared, the needs of most if not all students with special needs could be met in general education.

The idea of involving general education teachers in teaching students with special needs, referred to then as mainstreaming and today as inclusion, is an accepted part of educational practice today. Then, as now, a key assumption is that general education teachers can be prepared to effectively teach students with special needs and that such teaching can be successfully carried out in the general education classroom. Over the years, research on the question of the effectiveness of inclusion has been mixed. Bill was to learn in his schools in Vermont that meeting the needs of students with reading problems and disabilities in the general education classroom is hard work.

As already described, Bill's approach to reading instruction had consisted of conscientiously following the school basal reading program, providing extra practice with worksheets, and motivating students to read through games and library books of interest. Now, Bill was teaching reading by applying the DABIME model. ABA reading interventions involved a high percentage of decoding instruction. The emphasis on word identification was in many ways reflective of the times. While there was considerable disagreement about the role of phonics, instruction in reading comprehension was not a major focus in general. The underlying assumption was that if children could be successfully taught to decode, comprehension would naturally follow.

At face value, this assumption about the importance of fluent word reading does have some validity as most struggling readers do have problems with word identification. Research has also shown that estimates of the number of "word callers," those who can decode fluently without being able to comprehend, tend to be overestimated (Meisinger, Bradley, Schwanenflugel, Kuhn, & Morris, 2009). However, it is now commonly accepted that fluent decoding is necessary but not sufficient for reading comprehension. Comprehension requires competence with all aspects of language, not just those associated with phonology and its written language counterpart, phonics.

The key is whether essential reading content in both decoding and comprehension is taught systematically and explicitly enough so it can be readily learned. It is also fair to say that part of the reason for the emphasis on phonics was that it was a good fit for ABA. Phonics skills could be readily task analyzed, sequenced, observed, measured, and taught to mastery using repeated practice, reading comprehension less so. That said, behaviorism did provide Bill with the comfort of having a specific, effective strategy for teaching hard-to-teach children to decode words fluently. This was an important teaching practice that Bill had lacked until that time and that was conspicuously absent from his teacher education classes in Buffalo.

Year 2 of the CT program consisted of an internship in a Vermont school district. As agreed to upon entry into the program, interns were to spend at least two years in a school district following an internship in that district during the second year of the program. After a stressful interview process in which he and his fellow interns competed for the same limited number of positions throughout the state, Bill landed in Manchester, Vermont, a picturesque resort town just down the mountain from several Southern Vermont ski resorts.

Given his status as an outsider, Bill was warned by his advisor not to say that he would be servicing children, because in Vermont you serviced cows! What Bill was unprepared for was the negativity associated with his newfound behaviorism. Among the first interview questions he was accusingly asked was, "Are you a Skinnerian?"

Policy experts emphasize that school reform needs to be carefully aligned with the goals of the community to be effective. While it seemed that the state of Vermont and the CT program were very much aligned, it became clear to Bill at his interview that the schools were less so. Bill's district was reimbursed by the state for most of his salary as a CT, and that, not philosophical agreement, was likely the primary district motivator.

In retrospect, Bill felt he was viewed more as an extra teacher who came cheap than as the change agent he prepared to be. To illustrate, after describing the program to one of his school boards during his first year in the district, Bill was asked if the purpose of the program was to create articulate window washers. This was the same school that fought the addition of ramps for a student with physical disabilities for aesthetic reasons. While the state of Vermont had a law in place for several years requiring education for students with disabilities, PL 94-142 had also just been passed. Needless to say, Bill realized right away that he had his work cut out for him.

Bill was assigned to five rural schools. Two of the schools were small—K-8 buildings. The other three schools consisted of one or two grades in a single, small building. One school housed a single K-1 class on top of a mountain (quite difficult to reach in the winter with Bill's orange Volkswagen bus!). It wasn't long before Bill began to appreciate the advice of his former colleague in Buffalo who warned about the difficulties involved in changing adult behavior.

The CT model was one of indirect service. Bill's job was to teach general education teachers to apply DABIME to serving their students who struggled to learn and/or behave. The training was to be accomplished in two ways: (1) day-to-day, on-site consultation; and (2) graduate-level classes offered to teachers in their local schools. Teachers who enrolled in and successfully completed the classes earned graduate credit from the University of Vermont.

The CT program's emphasis on providing professional development through ongoing consultation and graduate classes offered in the schools was quite innovative at the time, but there were problems with the model as well. The content of the classes consisted almost exclusively of ABA. This was most helpful in measuring students' progress and building student social behaviors.

ABA was less helpful in academic areas. The assumption was that teachers would automatically apply the behavioral principles to reading. In reality, teachers lacked knowledge of the essential reading content needed to do that, content that included key elements of both decoding and comprehension. Also, when teachers tried to apply ABA to reading, they tended to gravitate to behaviors that could be more readily measured such as word identification and ignore behaviors that were not, such as reading comprehension.

One of Bill's roles as a CT was to help establish what was called district minimum objectives in reading and math. Minimum objectives were essential academic outcomes that all students were expected to attain—not everything taught, but foundational academic skills that all students needed to learn to be successful in school. The minimum objectives differed from today's standards that represent more general curricular guidelines rather than specific academic outcomes.

Each objective was constructed so that it could be observed and measured, allowing student progress to be monitored systematically. Progress monitoring helped make decisions about which students Bill would serve and whether the services he provided were successful.

Unlike the standards and high-stakes assessments of today, the minimum objectives were selected and designed by the teachers themselves under the guidance of Bill and his fellow CT colleague who was also working in the district. As a classroom teacher in Buffalo, Bill always had the nagging notion that his teaching lacked a clear focus. In Vermont, he felt strongly that minimum objectives were providing his teachers with such a focus. Ultimately, minimum objectives systems and others like them were abandoned, criticized for setting the bar too low.

We may currently be in a period where we are setting the bar too high. The *No Child Left Behind* goal of all children becoming readers was never reached and common core and other state standards remain high, so high that recently even soccer moms have been complaining about them. Maybe the Goldilocks effect will occur and educators will eventually get it "just right." Nonetheless, this early experience with minimum objectives had a major impact on Bill professionally, setting the stage for later work he was to do as a teacher educator in the area of curriculum-based assessment, and, most recently, response to intervention (RTI).

The federal role in education had increased with the passing of Title 1 in 1965, but money earmarked for districts came with few strings attached other than it be used with low-income children. In Bill's district, Title 1 reading was mainly carried out using a pull-out model. In a pull-out model, the Title 1 teacher serves students in small groups in a setting other than the general education classroom.

Pull-out programs allowed services to be provided to children with minimal disruption to the ongoing general education program. However, the pull-out approach made it difficult for Bill to carry out his program. He required classroom teachers to actually change what they were doing, a tall order under any set of circumstances, but especially when other support persons weren't requiring teachers to change anything!

One of the Title 1 teachers employed a language experience approach similar to what Bill had used unsuccessfully in Buffalo. He used the students' oral language to make books, which then became the students' readers. While this approach was no more successful in Vermont than in Buffalo, the idea of children publishing their own books combined with the fact that he, like the other Title 1 teacher, did not require teachers to change their teaching was positively received by teachers.

Also factors at least in the eyes of Bill, was that the other Title 1 teacher had the cache' and the instant credibility of a Ph.D. As a teacher in Buffalo, Bill would often refer to a person with a Ph.D. as a Pretentious Honky Dude. Not any more! Seeing how people in the field were responding to this Title 1 teacher, along with the fact that Bill's professors in the CT program were beginning to encourage their CTs to get doctorates, Bill began to approach the idea of Ph.D. differently. While he remained in Vermont for two more years to fulfill his service obligation, the decision had been made. Bill was going to get a Ph.D., a move that would change the path he took for the remainder of his career.

DIRECT INSTRUCTION: WHERE HAVE YOU BEEN ALL MY LIFE?

In the spring of 1976, the CT program sent all the interns to the annual International Conference of the Council for Exceptional Children in Atlanta. This was Bill's first professional conference, and it was to have a lasting impact on his subsequent work in Vermont and beyond. As already said, ABA was exhilarating for Bill after all those years in Buffalo without a concrete idea for how to teach struggling learners effectively. Bill's teaching epiphany became complete in Atlanta, where he had his first contact with Direct Instruction (DI), the use of the upper-case letters DI denoting curriculum materials designed according to principles initially developed by Siegfried Engelmann, then of the University of Oregon.

Bill attended a presentation given by Doug Carnine, a former student of Engelmann and also a professor at Oregon. He was impressed with the results of a research study Carnine presented that showed positive results for DI with the same urban students with whom Bill had been largely ineffective in Buffalo. DI was one of the basic skills models in the Follow Through experiment and Carnine presented preliminary results showing that DI had been the most effective of all the models. What became clear to Bill more than ever after hearing Carnine's presentation was that hard-to-teach students could be effectively taught to read if their instruction was carefully designed and delivered. Bill returned to his district energized and committed to learning more about DI and introducing it into his schools.

What impressed Bill the most about DI was the careful way it taught children to read. DI was the first program in all of his years of teaching that designed instruction in such a way as to prevent many of the learning problems he had previously encountered with his students. It had always bothered Bill that students would consistently guess at words instead of trying to systematically figure them out. They would look at the words around an unknown word, the pictures, the teacher, doing everything but carefully examining the word itself.

DI, also called *Direct Instruction System for Teaching Reading (DISTAR)*, focused on teaching students how to figure out words independently without guessing. The program prevented guessing by teaching students a systematic *strategy* for figuring out words by themselves. Students were taught to identify the most common sounds of written letters, break words into their component sounds, and blend sounds together to form words. This is now referred to as systematic, explicit phonemic awareness and phonics, but Engelmann never called it that. He was a philosopher before he was an educator, and the design of DI was driven by logically determining what it took to read independently.

DI also reinforced strategic word reading by carefully attending to important details such as eliminating student dependence on using pictures to decode words. The program presented pictures only *after* students had read a passage. Its scripted teaching formats, though frequently frowned upon by the educational establishment, ensured that errors were corrected in such a way as to reinforce student sounding skills.

The program required students to sound out the entire missed word, rather than just telling them the word or encouraging them to guess at the word using the context and first sound. Of course, students were only asked to sound out words that *could* be sounded out and for which they had been previously taught the sounds, further evidence of DI's attention to important design details.

The features of DI's carefully designed instruction, previously missing from Bill's teaching preparation and experience, were also effectively used in DI to teach the other key parts of reading including fluency, vocabulary, oral language, and comprehension. To someone like Bill, desperately searching for something that worked, the DI design and scripts were inviting; there was no guesswork involved, and planning consisted mainly of rehearsal as opposed to creating new lessons. The fun was in watching children learn who had previously failed.

At the time, DI seemed to be everything Bill had been looking for in a program to teach at-risk students and students with disabilities to read. He wrote a state grant to procure *DISTAR* reading materials and taught himself to use the scripted formats that summer with a small group of previously unsuccessful third graders in one of his schools. Bill practiced the scripted formats with his wife Beth playing the students before introducing his daily lessons. The students took to the instruction well; for the first time in their lives, they felt successful in reading. This initial success led to the need for a major decision as to how to continue the program in the fall.

Because Bill was only present one day per week in the school where he had started DI that summer, someone other than he had to teach the program. Bill had two options: either prepare the classroom teacher to do it or use pull-out and train a paraprofessional. His CT background dictated that he train the classroom teacher to carry it out. Bill's mentors at the university had known that pull-out was easier and that it would be a tempting option for the interns. Because of this, they had strongly discouraged providing services that exempted the classroom teacher from responsibility.

An indirect services approach did have several advantages. Pull-out requires that the students would have to be pulled out of something. If the teacher implemented the program, the students wouldn't need to miss any instruction. Also, once the teacher was able to carry out the program, she could use it to help other students in the future who may have similar problems.

That said, Bill's experience with Title 1 in his first year in the district had taught him that pull-out was easier because it didn't require teachers to change what they were doing. Besides, Bill felt he lacked the political clout to leverage teacher behavior and had learned that the soft sell could only get him so far. Selling DI to the classroom teacher, with its scripted formats and careful attention to detail, would be difficult. Bill was also naturally averse to conflict and short on conflict resolution skills.

In the end, unable to resist the pull-out temptation, Bill chose the paraprofessional route and was able to get the state to fund a part-time paraprofessional. The result was positive. The students continued to make great progress, the paraprofessional carried out the program impeccably, and she loved doing it. Bill was to eventually employ the same approach in all of his other schools but one using DI delivered by a state-funded paraprofessional. While he continued to provide consultation services to his classroom teachers, the emphasis of the program had changed direction, from providing indirect services by training the teacher to serving students directly using DI delivered by a paraprofessional.

There are educators today who object to paraprofessionals being responsible for teaching new or initial skills. Bill's experience shows that with careful training and a carefully designed reading program, it can be done successfully. Of course, the downside was that Bill's general education teachers lacked a tool that could have helped them with other present and future hard-to-teach students.

One of Bill's schools was different because it consisted only of one K-1 class and was located in a rural community at the summit of one of the Green Mountains. The teacher had concerns about the reading progress of one particular student. Bill was unable to justify funding a paraprofessional for only one student and thus the classroom teacher was the only option. Theoretically, this case was ideally suited for the CT model of indirect services. Unfortunately, that's not what the teacher thought. She felt she had already tried everything and that the student needed something beyond what she could provide. Bill had her attempt a series of behavioral interventions but without success.

Were the interventions ineffective because she didn't think they would be or because the student needed a more intensive intervention that was either beyond her expertise or not feasible for her to deliver? In reality, it was probably a little bit of both. Consulting services may be adequate for some students, but others may need a more direct, intensive approach.

One year later, when Bill had already left the district to pursue doctoral studies halfway across the country, this same teacher mailed him a pile of this student's papers, pointing out that he had still not made progress. Evidently, she continued to blame Bill. The matter of how to effectively provide interventions of varying intensity, or differentiated instruction, in general education classrooms remains an issue all these years later.

In the fall of Bill's final year in Vermont, the state held what was one of the several public hearings conducted throughout the state on the status of special education in Vermont. Several of Bill's professors from the CT program attended. Bill was called on to describe his program. He knew he had deviated significantly from the CT program's model of indirect service and worried about the reaction of his former teachers. Ultimately their approval didn't matter. In the spring of 1978, Bill was accepted into the doctoral program at the University of Illinois at Urbana-Champaign, where he was to study under a professor whose research in reading Bill had greatly admired.

It is important to say that the CT program was eventually revised based on experiences, such as Bill's. Later versions of the program included more systematic training on specific methods of professional development and systems change, areas that had been particularly difficult for him. Perhaps with more extensive training in these areas, Bill would have been better able to implement the model. All of this aside, he left Vermont much farther on the road to knowing how to effectively teach students to read than when he started. As Bill wrote in his application letter for graduate school:

> My experiences in Vermont have convinced me that definite educational gains can be made. I have trained teachers and a staff of five paraprofessionals to carry our direct instructional programs based on the principles of task and concept analysis, reinforcement theory, and data-based classroom decision making. The results in terms of measurable pupil growth in the basic skill areas of reading and math have been gratifying.

Nonetheless, Bill realized that he had much more to learn. While he had been able to prepare paraprofessionals to teach DI effectively, his record of teaching teachers was not nearly as successful. Bill felt that a doctoral degree would provide him with the skills and the opportunity to more effectively teach teachers. As also stated in his letter of application:

> I hope to reach my eventual goal of helping our schools to better meet the needs of handicapped learners by training those who teach them in the most effective means available.

Upon leaving the district, Bill's curriculum coordinator, a former nun turned public school administrator, displaying a worried look on her face, asked Bill whether he was going to write about the district when he left. At the time, Bill was too excited about the future to dwell on the past. Now, forty-five years later, retired, but still trying to sort things out, he is glad to be doing just that.

REFLECTION

Reflecting back today on these early experiences, as well as the themes identified in chapter 1, it seems that despite higher societal expectations during this period as to the importance of literacy, there didn't seem to be an equivalent level of urgency when it came to classroom practice. Activist advocacy stressing the importance of reading for personal empowerment was present in the Black community in Buffalo and given considerable lip service in the Teacher Corps program. There were also multiple federal programs in the process of being implemented such as Title 1 and Follow Through programs designed specifically to level the playing field for students living in poverty.

Nonetheless, there was a definite disconnect between community expectations for empowerment and day-to-day reading instruction. That instruction consisted of the school basal supplemented with a language experience approach, and a heavy dose of motivational activities, mainly games, approaches that had largely failed to be validated by research conducted at the time. Federal programs were either untested, such as the responsive teaching model employed in Bill's third grade Follow Through class, or were in the form of extra instruction, but with no requirements for what that instruction should include.

Unlike today, no high-stakes testing program was in place, yet it couldn't have been more clear that the students in Bill's school couldn't read very well. While, in general, his intentions were good, Bill's overarching concern as a beginning teacher was classroom management, a topic that had been largely missing from his college classes. Bill was in survival mode as he filled much of his instructional time with activities designed to keep his students happy and in their seats. No liberation or eradication of poverty there.

It is noteworthy that Bill seems to blame the ignorance of effective practices as being responsible for the disconnect between community aspirations and instructional practice, and certainly, that was a likely part of the problem. However, a case could also be made for the presence of race and class issues. How high exactly were Bill's expectations, really? Would he have been accepting low achievement if the students had been white middle-class children from his community? Had staff internalized the *Coleman Report* and felt powerless in the face of poverty? Did they expect less because black lives didn't matter as much as white lives? The fact that we continue to grapple with these problems today is disappointing, though also testimony to the complexity of the problem at hand.

Bill's early experiences as a teacher brought him directly within the sphere of influence of the basal reader, which, at this time, was already a widespread part of the educational system. While supplements were allowed, alternatives were rarely even a consideration. As Chall pointed out at the time, publishers had assumed the role of experts, made possible at least in part by a general lack of information on effective practices on the part of teachers such as Bill and principals.

As a teacher, Bill sensed a major reading problem but didn't know what to do about it. For him, the basal was a lifesaver because it readily filled a reading information void. Unfortunately, the basals at the time had yet to incorporate adequately the latest reading research recommended by Chall and others.

Fortunately, Bill's special education preparation and experience in Vermont provided him with a much-needed change of professional direction. Special educators tend to gravitate toward instruction that is more explicit and systematic because instruction for students with disabilities is much less forgiving than teaching students without disabilities. By definition, most students with disabilities don't learn from the standard instructional fare, including the basal reader.

Bill's unsuccessful teaching experience in Buffalo also made him more receptive to the need for careful instruction for educationally disadvantaged children. ABA and DI provided much-needed guidance for Bill and his commitment to them at the time bordered on apostolic. After six years of doubt in Buffalo, Bill thought he had found the answer to solving reading problems, though as he was to learn the hard way, not all educators are similarly inclined. Indeed, effective teaching may be necessary for solving the achievement gap but is certainly not sufficient.

Bill was able to credibly teach himself to carry out DI effectively, convincing teachers to do it was another thing altogether. General educators tend to give more weight to motivational teaching strategies and can perceive structure as evidence of a lack of creativity. Witness the cool reception the findings of project Follow Through received in chapters 1 and 2, and the "drill and kill" mantra often associated with DI. The difficulties in finding just the right balance between motivation and explicit, systematic teaching were to be a recurrent theme in Bill's future work as a teacher educator in higher education.

Chapter 4

Teaching Reading 1983–2008
Reading Policy Takes Center Stage

As covered in chapter 1, the period from 1955 to 1983 saw the decline and fall of look-say, the whole word method of reading instruction that characterized much of the first half of the twentieth century. This decline was largely brought about by research findings at the time that had drawn two major conclusions: (a) reading instruction should include a combination of systematic, explicit phonics and comprehension and (b) setting and teacher factors are important to consider.

As explained in chapter 2, those who were phonics advocates tended to stress the first finding, and those favoring an approach that emphasized comprehension while de-emphasizing decoding tended to stress the second. This development set the stage for three decades of reading wars at a time when reading instruction became an important part of a national education policy debate. The major components of that debate are recounted in this chapter.

FAUX PHONICS

Throughout the 1970s and as the 1980s arrived, phonics was playing a greater role than it had during the look-say-dominated 1950s and 1960s. As Pearson (1999) has pointed out, however, the method of teaching phonics was much like the phonics of old. It remained within a basal format, was neither systematic nor explicit, and was only repositioned to appear earlier than in the look-say basals that preceded it.

The 1970s also saw the rise of phonics worksheets, whose use had become widespread in the 1970s. This development was at least partly due to the popularity of *mastery learning*. The idea behind mastery learning was that: (1) complex skills could be broken down into manageable parts; (2) performance on these parts could be assessed using classroom-based tests; and (3) students would normally move through the parts, one at a time, in succession, until learning was attained. Given the appropriate skill sequence and time, learning was viewed as inevitable. The phrase "all children can learn" was popularized during this period.

The emergence of mastery learning dovetailed well with the task analytic, ABA approach that came into prominence in the 1960s and 1970s, particularly in special education. It was also consistent with Chall's call for more systematic phonics in basal reading programs, as phonics lent itself well to the process of breaking skills down into their components. However, an unintended consequence of mastery learning on reading instruction was the increased use of supplementary phonics worksheets.

The problem with worksheets is that phonics is an oral task while written worksheets are not. This instructional mismatch, later termed by Heward, Damer, and Wood (2004) as faux phonics, refers to any phonics activity that is either soundless (e.g., students circle the letter that begins with the same sound as a picture) or letter-less (e.g., students say rhyming words in the presence of no letters). The phonics worksheets of the 1970s were also notorious for not being coordinated with words students found in their reading books, as well as having complicated, multistep directions. While these workbook activities may have kept students busy, they did little to help them apply phonics skills to reading words.

In this way, Chall's call for systematic, explicit early phonics was compromised, leaving phonics instruction vulnerable to criticism and the reading field open to the adoption of other approaches. Also of note during this period were the results of classroom observations of reading instruction in grades 3–6 made by Durkin (1978–1979), who found that very little classroom time was being devoted to *teaching* reading, reading comprehension in particular. According to Durkin's findings, most instructional time was spent on written assignments that simply asked students comprehension questions without teaching them how to answer them.

THE EMERGENCE OF NATIONAL SCHOOL REFORM

In the 1960s and 1970s, there was the usual ebb and flow of new reading teaching ideas such as language experience and mastery learning. These discussions, except for Flesch's *Why Johnny Can't Read*, took place primarily within the educational community and did not involve the public at large in general and public policymakers in particular. Since the *Coleman Report* of the 1960s, which held parental and community background as the primary driver of school achievement, the public seemed generally content with the

Title 1 compensatory model of providing funding to the individual student rather than school level. In this way, day-to-day school operations remained untouched.

One sign of change to come became known as the Effective Schools Movement (Edmonds, 1979). Edmonds decried the lack of equity in our school systems as demonstrated by what we now refer to as the achievement gap between poor and middle-class children. Further, Edmonds promoted the idea that there was no excuse for not doing anything about this gap because some schools, what Edmonds called "effective schools," were in effect already doing it. Edmonds identified and studied these successful high-poverty schools and compiled a list of teaching strategies that all schools could use to shrink the gap between the rich and poor children.

The qualities identified by Edmonds included effective leadership, a clear and focused mission, a safe and orderly environment, a climate of high expectations, frequent monitoring of student progress, and positive home-school relations. The no-excuses attitude and the use of evidence-based practices of the Effective Schools Movement foreshadowed the No Child Left Behind Act of 2002. As reflected in other later Title 1 reauthorizations, funding also began to be tied to operations at the *school* rather than the student level.

While the Effective Schools Movement was an important forerunner to school reform, the generally recognized birth of the current school reform movement came when the Reagan administration published *A Nation at Risk* in 1983. This document was to make education policy an economic issue, arguing that our economic woes were due to what the report referred to as "a rising level of mediocrity" in our students that amounted to "committing an act of unthinking, unilateral, educational disarmament."

The original purpose for writing the report had been to support Reagan's goals for prayer in schools, voucher programs, and the abolishment of the Department of Education itself. There was also little actual evidence for the supposition that the nation was at risk because of low academic achievement. Nonetheless, the report resonated with the public, making front-page news and planting the seeds for a school reform movement that continues to this day. For example, it is hard to find an article about the achievement gap in reading, this book included, without an opening paragraph proclaiming the economic consequences of reading problems, both to the individual and our country as a whole.

THE WHOLE LANGUAGE ERA

With the publication of *Becoming a Nation of Readers* in 1985, matters related to reading instruction also began to take on more of a national flavor.

Since the 1960s, a considerable amount of reading research had been conducted and there was a perceived need in the field for a synthesis of its findings. As written in its abstract, this federally funded report reached two main conclusions that were remarkably similar to those reached by Edmonds: (1) that "the knowledge is now available to make worthwhile improvements in reading throughout the United States" and (2) "if the practices seen in the best classrooms in the best schools could be introduced everywhere, improvement in reading would be dramatic."

Regarding specific teaching practices, the report stands out for two reasons. First, it struck a balance among many aspects of reading including "well-designed phonics instruction" along with oral language, comprehension, and written expression. Second, as Pearson (1999) noted, while the report was balanced in its attention to reading practices, it did signal a shift from viewing reading as a perceptual, primarily word identification activity to one whose primary purpose was comprehension.

Becoming a Nation of Readers appeared to strike a reasonable balance between the teaching of word reading (including phonics) and comprehending oral and written languages. Still, its impact on the reading community at large was minimal. Indeed, a storm was brewing in educational circles across the country and its name was the *Whole Language Movement*. Whole language had its origins in the 1960s through the 1970s as research on reading expanded to other fields such as psychology, sociology, linguistics, and psycholinguistics, and increasingly focused on comprehension as opposed to word identification (Pearson, 1999).

The founders and primary movers of the *Whole Language Movement* were Kenneth and Yetta Goodman (Goodman & Goodman, 1979) and Frank Smith (1971). Whole language was promoted as a philosophy rather than a distinct set of practices as in the conventional wisdom about teaching reading of the day.

The basic idea of whole language was that given a literature-rich environment, and a purpose for reading, children learn to read as naturally as they learned to speak and understand oral language. It was the teacher's role to arrange the classroom environment in such a way that reading would develop naturally. The emphasis in whole language was on performing authentic reading tasks, not the prepackaged basal lessons and activities of the past.

A key feature responsible for the meteoric rise of whole language in the 1980s was its political element. An important part of whole language was teacher empowerment. Unlike the basal reading lessons that were prescribed by experts, the goal of whole language was to ensure that "teachers are not relying on gurus and experts to tell them what to do" (Goodman cited in Kim, 2008, p. 98). According to Goodman, the *Whole Language Movement* was generating a knowledge-base "passed from teacher-to-teacher in person contacts, in teacher support groups, and in local conferences" (Goodman cited in Kim, 2008, p. 98).

Not surprisingly, teachers loved whole language. Such was its popularity that a 1992 survey conducted by the NAEP showed that "42% of teachers reported a 'heavy' emphasis on whole language and an additional 41% reported a 'moderate' emphasis" (Stahl, 1999, p. 15). While some of these numbers were because the basal readers at the time had incorporated whole language into their materials, nonetheless, it was popular enough for some researchers to declare that whole language had become the new conventional wisdom (Pearson, 1999).

The rise of whole language reached its peak in 1987 with the passage of the California State Language Arts Framework, which established a statewide, literature-based, whole language approach. Its rather sudden fall from favor corresponds roughly with the publication of NAEP reading scores at the state level in 1992. Before that time, the performance of individual states on the NAEP was not reported.

With the change in policy, states were able to not only see how they had done individually but were also able to compare their performance with other states. California found that its 1992 scores lagged behind the other most highly populated states of New York, Texas, and Florida. Its 1994 scores were still lower, with California fourth graders performing among the lowest in the country. According to Kim, in California, "on the 1994 NAEP, 56 percent of fourth graders read below basic, including 46 percent of families with college-educated parents" (2008, p. 99).

While the poor performance of students in California was likely due to multiple factors, the pieces were certainly in place for whole language to take the blame as it had been prominently and publicly supported there. Whole language had also planted the seeds of its own destruction. Its backers emphasized the importance of student motivation, often at the expense of the direct teaching of basic reading skills such as phonics and phonemic awareness. By doing so, they ignored an ever-increasing body of research verifying their importance.

Whole language's rejection of traditional instruction also led its backers to dismiss or ignore other frequently used (and effective) components of reading instruction such as independent learning strategy instruction, student use of text structure and background knowledge to comprehend text, and reading in the content areas. The neglect of these more traditional and often necessary aspects of literacy instruction reduced its support among more moderate researchers and practitioners who were not willing to give up teaching strategies they had found to be successful in the past (Pearson, 1999).

In addition, whole language's unchecked support of teacher empowerment made using a systematic approach to professional development difficult. If you say the teacher always knows best, it is hard to justify activities designed to boost teacher competence. The neglect of professional development led to questionable applications of whole language such as an overemphasis on large-group instruction.

Those who favored whole language also downplayed the importance of measurable academic results at a time when the drumbeat for school accountability in the form of higher test scores was just beginning to be heard. Part of this dismissal of test scores was due to the whole language's research base that tended to look to ways to verify teaching effectiveness other than test scores.

However, at the same time, the National Institute of Child Health and Development (NICHD) was engaging in its own brand of reading research, which was more compatible with the societal trend of accountability-based reform based on standardized test scores. Of all these factors, the refusal to honor test scores was perhaps the most damning. In the end, the whole language advocates could show no gains for the children who needed them most: children who were at risk or who had disabilities. These students needed a different approach.

The question then at the dawn of the twentieth century was: What direction literacy instruction would take? Would the reading community be able to juggle the multiple goals of motivation, word identification, and reading comprehension and come up with an approach that met student needs in all three of these areas? Would the pendulum swing back to a phonics first approach, neglecting or at least de-emphasizing other critical areas of reading instruction?

READING REFORM GOES NATIONAL

In 1998, The National Research Council, part of the National Academy of Sciences, issued a 390-page report synthesizing the literature to date on effective ways to teach reading. Like *Becoming a Nation of Readers* and *Learning to Read: The Great Debate* before it, the report supported the necessity of phonics in early reading instruction, but within a total reading program that also stressed oral and written language. At the time, some in the popular press heralded this development and even declared an end to the reading wars. Unfortunately, the Council's report only served to fuel the next volley in what has proven to be a stubborn conflict.

In the late 1990s, the problem perceived by the public was one of lower achievement in reading. As discussed earlier, in the early to mid-1990s, the results of the NAEP in several states were showing a general downward trend in reading, and, at the time, the use of whole language was so widespread it was being referred to as the "conventional wisdom" in reading instruction.

An approach doesn't become the conventional wisdom without alienating those who favor other methods of teaching reading. Ironically, while whole language teachers essentially determined their own individual approaches to teaching it, at the same time, they adhered to a doctrinaire approach that left little to no room for other ways to teach, especially phonics instruction. Many whole language advocates viewed phonics as generally unnatural and unnecessary.

There were political forces at play, largely comprising backers of phonics instruction who were well placed in the political system and highly motivated to make significant changes in policy. In addition to the NAEP results, phonics advocates were armed with the results of research conducted in the 1990s by the NICHD showing that early interventions in reading that included systematic and explicit instruction in phonics could reduce reading failure (Lyon & Fletcher, 2001).

Added to this was a high-stakes testing environment that was just peaking, as well as the increased use of mandated curriculum to ensure that teaching policies were adequately carried out. Finally, and unfortunately, policy decisions in general often tend to come down to either-or, yes-or-no decisions, with nuance usually taking a back seat. So much for the end of the reading wars!

By 1999, thirty-six states had bills passed or that were pending promoting the use of phonics instruction and including professional development for educators on how to teach it. At the same time, Congress felt the need for another research synthesis, one based exclusively on high-quality experimental research. The purpose of the report was to make explicit, scientifically based recommendations about reading instruction to classroom teachers. Hence, in 2000, a panel of experts, the *NRP*, was assembled to compile such a report.

The *NRP* employed a rigorous process in selecting research studies, only including ones that met high methodological standards that panel members made clear and public. The goal was to establish guidelines for teaching reading that was to be commonly referred to as "scientifically based reading instruction" or SBRI. The *NRP*'s conclusions were based on the best science available at the time. Its actual findings, however, were not significantly different from those of previous reviews. The *NRP* concluded that systematic, explicit instruction in phonemic awareness and phonics, particularly at younger ages, was necessary for teaching children to read though by no means sufficient. Instruction must also include teaching in the areas of fluency, vocabulary, and comprehension.

The original purpose for assembling the *NRP* had been to settle the question of what was the best way to teach reading once and for all, a noble, yet difficult, if not impossible, task. The *NRP* did identify five key areas of reading instruction including phonemic awareness, phonics, fluency, vocabulary, and comprehension. The identification of these five areas was intended to keep teachers' focus on a comprehensive approach to reading instruction, rather than to a single area.

Eerily similar to responses to earlier research syntheses, most researchers and policymakers exercised what Cooper (2005) referred to as "theory creep" when interpreting the *NRP*'s findings. They viewed the *NRP* glass as either half full or half empty depending on their preexisting beliefs about reading instruction. Phonics advocates tended to emphasize its scientific rigor and its confirmation of the importance of teacher-centered instruction, particularly in the areas of phonics and phonemic awareness.

Whole language advocates and numerous members of the traditional literacy establishment decried its narrow scope, its inclusion of only quantitative research studies in the findings, and vested panel interests. Critics also accused the panel of misrepresenting its findings in a widely disseminated executive summary of the report. Shanahan (2003), a member of the *NRP*, has largely refuted these criticisms, while also making the point that the critics found fault with its process, including what it did not do, not with its major findings.

THE GREAT READING FIRST EXPERIMENT

Perhaps the most significant effect of the *NRP* was that its findings were used by Congress to guide the design of Reading First (RF). RF represented the culmination of reform-minded federal policies dating back to the 1994 reauthorization of Title 1. That 1994 Bill set the stage for an era of accountability, with states setting learning standards, developing assessments to measure their attainment, and setting policies specifically related to reading. It also led to legislative efforts such as The America Reads Act of 1997 and the Reading Excellence Act of 1998.

RF was funded as part of the No Child Left Behind Act (NCLB) of 2001, a revision of the ESEA that mandated school accountability for student outcomes in reading and math based on yearly standardized tests. NCLB was approved by both liberals and conservatives, as part of a post 9/11 wave of bipartisanship. NCLB satisfied conservatives' desire to hold schools accountable for results and liberals' desire to narrow the achievement gap. In funding RF, Congress: (1) agreed that there was a reading problem; (2) agreed that the problem could be solved using scientifically based reading practices that included systematic phonics instruction; and (3) made policy to bring about their agreed-upon solution (U.S. Department of Education, 2002).

The purpose of RF was "to give teachers across the nation the skills they needed to teach all children to read fluently by the end of third grade." Viewed from the perspective of today's legislative gridlock, the passage of RF was an amazing occurrence. Even though the Reading Excellence Act that preceded it also received a generous level of funding, and required recipients to restrict their reading instruction to practices that were "scientifically based," the RF requirements for receiving that money were more specific than ever before.

To be funded, state plans needed to (1) include systematic methods in all five areas of reading as laid out by the *NRP*; (2) use rigorous data analysis procedures by employing technically proven assessments; and (3) be based on studies published in peer-reviewed publications. RF was a far cry from the early days of Title 1 when money was handed out with no requirements other than it be used with disadvantaged children.

The fact that RF specified curriculum content and steered programs to adopt specific assessment systems was also quite different, as prior Title 1 reauthorizations had always left such decisions up to the states and local districts. Past policy legislation also considered other sources of information during development such as "expert testimony from practitioners, information about school organization and finance, and evaluation of compelling cases" (Coburn, Pearson, & Woulfin, 2011, p. 564). RF was designed to be based only on methodologically sound research as defined by the *NRP*.

However, with greater specificity comes greater scrutiny. While the research base for RF was extensive, it was far from complete. For example, the benefits of several key features of RF such as decodable (phonetically based) practice books, the technical adequacy of its progress monitoring assessments, and coaching as an instrument of professional development had yet to be firmly established. Such ambiguities in the research base made implementation of the law difficult and left it vulnerable to criticism.

Perhaps more critically, for a field normally used to adopting ready-made, commercially produced programs to bring about change, only two programs—Direct Instruction and *Success for All*, the latter a nonprofit product of the whole schools reform movement of the 1990s—met the legislation's very specific guidelines for being scientifically based.

Faced with traditional Congressional concerns about local control of education, as well as the logistics of implementing a nationwide project with only two programs meeting criteria for being scientific, RF changed the criteria. Now, programs didn't have to be *validated directly* by well-designed research; they just had to be *aligned with existing research* in the five aspects of reading as defined in the *NRP*. As a result of the change in criteria, five programs "based on research" were added to the RF list of "acceptable" programs, some of which had ties to the RF reading consultants.

Chapter 4

As discussed in chapters 2 and 3, DI had a history going back to the late 1960s and early 1970s when it was one of the models in the Project Follow Through experiment. Despite the fact that a number of the statistical analyzes favored the DI model, the educational establishment at the time was put off by DI's highly structured, scripted teaching approach and downplayed its impact.

The response to this interpretation of the findings from the DI implementers was, and remains to this day, "We got robbed!" The point here is that while they didn't write RF (Reid Lyon of NICHD and Robert Sweet, a veteran House Education Committee staffer did), many of these same DI players and their direct descendants were actively involved in its formation from the beginning. RF was their chance to finally balance the scales and implement their approach on a national stage.

Establishing the control required to implement a program as prescriptive as RF proved to be very difficult. Stern (2008) related that

> Department of Education officials in Washington were being tasked with supervising 50 separate state Reading First programs, each with its own procedures for getting approved reading materials. The central staff also had to make sure that each state conducted initial training in reading science and then continued professional development and teacher training protocols into qualifying schools. Each of the states, in turn, was required to review the proposals of dozens of school districts and then monitor how the targeted schools were using a host of different reading programs. In addition, the Reading First office in Washington had to oversee regional technical assistance centers set up under the law, that, among their other tasks, were expected to provide guidance to the states about the many reading programs on the market and whether they qualified under the law's scientifically based reading research (SBRR) criteria. The central staff also had to make sure that each state conducted initial training in reading science and then continued professional development for the frontline teachers who were expected to deliver instruction in the classroom. (p. 22)

Astonishingly, the task of administering RF was originally left to only two people: Project Director Chris Doherty, who formerly directed a DI project in Baltimore, Maryland, and his deputy. While states did not have to name the programs they would use, their grant proposals needed to strictly adhere to the findings of the *NRP*, leading to many states having their grants initially rejected for not conforming to RF guidelines.

The Director, a strong advocate for the principles of DI, was determined to establish program fidelity. To assist with the process, two consultants from the University of Oregon, long a DI bastion, were contracted. At least seven others from Oregon assumed roles on committees to review reading materials to make sure they were aligned with the five elements of "scientifically based" reading instruction as laid out in the *NRP* (Glenn, 2007).

Ironically, with the addition of five programs to the list of programs considered acceptable by RF "experts," the two programs that were initially and solely acceptable, *Direct Instruction* and *Success for All*, were rarely chosen by states, leading Robert Slavin, the creator and head of *Success for All*, to question why his nonprofit program was being overlooked in favor of five as yet invalidated programs published by for-profit companies (Glenn, 2007). According to Stern:

> He (Slavin) issued a long formal complaint to the Department of Education and congressional committees, alleging that biased federal Reading First officials were responsible for Success for All's failure to be selected by more states and districts. Slavin charged that Reading First officials had conflicts of interest that led them to favor the products of some of the commercial publishers. (2008, p. 25)

When the Office of the Inspector General (OIG) looked into Slavin's complaint, it found that a number of those same University of Oregon consultants involved in helping states select and carry out scientifically based reading programs were involved in the publication of several of the approved programs they often recommended. This circumstance created at least the appearance of a conflict of interest.

However, Engelmann (2007), whose DI Program along with Slavin's was one of the overlooked programs, said that the consultants were just doing their job. He argued that three of the stated purposes of the RF law were to "provide assistance to state educational agencies and local educational agencies" in (1) establishing the reading programs for students in kindergarten through grade 3 that are based on scientifically based research; (2) selecting or administering screening, diagnostic, and classroom-based instructional reading assessments; and (3) selecting or developing effective instructional materials proven to prevent or remediate reading failure.

Engelmann pointed out that there is a fine line between interpreting such assistance as support for implementing the grant or an endorsement of a particular program. Such a nuanced position would unlikely be understood by legislators unfamiliar with the curriculum adoption process or ignored by competing, unapproved programs for the sake of their self-interest.

Nevertheless, as said by Slavin at the time, the consultants

> should have recused themselves from any role in advising states that were still in the process of building their Reading First packages. If they'd been government employees, this could have never happened. Because they were government

contractors, they somehow felt that these things didn't apply to them. (Glenn, 2007, p. 9)

Doherty was similarly criticized for preventing several states from adopting programs he thought did not follow SBRR as defined by the grant, which again, could be interpreted as just doing his job.

Perhaps most damning for Doherty, though, was a series of unflattering emails he wrote in which he referred to those complainants who favored curricula not on the accepted list as "dirtbags" who were "trying to crash our party" (Dillon, 2008). In another email, Doherty told a staff member to resist funding one particular program, saying "Beat the s..t out of them in a way that will stand up to any level of legal and [whole language] apologist scrutiny. Hit them over and over with definitive evidence that they are not SBRR, never have been, and never will be" (Stern, 2008, p. 27). Doherty was forced to resign in 2006, a victim of being overextended, careless, and naive as well as of national and reading politics.

HALF EMPTY OR HALF FULL ONCE MORE

While no wrong-doing was ever officially established, and preliminary results of RF up to that time had been positive, the damage had been done. By this time, the bipartisan coalition that passed RF in the first place had ceased to exist. The Iraq War and Hurricane Katrina had turned President Bush into a political target, rather than a partner. Democrats saw RF as one more way to denigrate President Bush, for whom RF had been one of the cornerstones of his administration. RF had entered the political realm, front and center!

Senator Edward Kennedy's comments about the RF situation represent well the political vise in which RF found itself:

> The Bush Administration has put cronyism first and the reading skills of our children last, and this report shows the disturbing consequences. Instead of awarding scarce dollars to reading programs that make a difference for our children, the administration chose to reward its friends instead. (Dillon, 2008)

Even President Bush and then Secretary of Education Margaret Spellings failed to come to RF's defense. In 2006, Congress cut 60 percent of RF's funding. The final nail in the RF coffin was waiting in the form of an impact study conducted by the Institute of Educational Sciences (IES) and published in 2008.

The IES is an "independent, non-partisan statistics, research and evaluation arm of the U.S. Department of Education. Its mission is to provide scientific evidence on which to ground education practice and policy" (Institute of Education Science, n.d.). IES conducted a research study on the impact of the RF package of assessments, intervention programs, and professional development on the reading achievement of children who had chronically underachieved in reading. The results of the study (Gamse, Jacob, Horst, Boulay, & Unlu, 2008) showed that RF schools carried out the key features of the RF program as proposed and exceeded control schools in decoding. There were no differences in reading comprehension at any grade level.

The RF Federal Advisory Committee took issue with the findings, claiming that the lack of differences could have resulted from the fact that the control and experimental groups were taken from the same districts, which often received the same professional development opportunities and used the same instructional materials. This claim had some merit, given the fact that RF required 1.25 billion of its allocated dollars be spent trying to get other schools to do what RF did, causing states such as Florida to implement RF statewide.

The committee also pointed out that the RF sample comprised only 2 percent of the total RF population and that the results of subgroups should have been reported. Last, the committee questioned why other reading outcomes such as fluency and vocabulary weren't considered, even though such information was available.

The results of state-level evaluations, which, by definition and necessity employed less rigorous research designs, with few exceptions, painted a different picture from the IES study. These studies showed increases in reading achievement, including comprehension, even among traditionally low-achieving groups. Most states also reported positive program changes and reading outcomes (Beck, 2010; Coburn et al., 2011). NAEP scores also rose significantly between 2002 and 2009, the years RF was implemented. However, as Pearson (2010) has pointed out, given the absence of strict experimental control, the positive state and national results could have at least partly been due to other factors such as the increased attention, resources, and focus that can result from a new project.

The mixed public reaction to the RF results was similar to reactions to all of the reading reports that preceded it. The "half empty" camp pointed out that the IES study was more scientific, and showed that RF had no impact on reading comprehension—the sine qua non of reading instruction. Beck (2010) has described this position as it relates to RF as, "Who cares if they can decode if they can't comprehend what they read" (p. 94). The half-empty approach usually leads to the all-too-common outcome of the project being dropped.

The "half full" group pointed to the positive state reports which, while not as scientific as the IES study, were data-based and promising nonetheless. As for the IES study, the students did improve in decoding, and, as Beck characterized this half-full position, "improved decoding puts a reader in position for improved comprehension *if* the other components (e.g. fluency, vocabulary) are in good shape or repaired."

A study by Coburn and Waulfin (2012) also found positive benefits for the teacher coaching in RF, a noteworthy accomplishment given that teacher behavior can be very resistant to change. As Coburn and Waulfin pointed out, teachers often undermine reform efforts by (1) rejecting them outright; (2) making a symbolic change so that only the appearance of change is created; (3) adding new practices but retaining ineffective ones; and (4) changing only superficial aspects of practice. In their study, the coaching in RF led teachers to "change deep, underlying beliefs and practices while taking on the message's beliefs and practices" (p. 30), not an easy thing to do. Finally, as Beck (2010) wrote, why not "build on what did work, or figure out why a component might not have worked, fix it and measure again" (2010, p. 94)?

The ultimate impact of RF is difficult to gauge. Certainly, there are thousands of educators nationwide who received many hours of successful professional development and are still teaching. Some evidence suggested that the project in at least two states was continuing, with student progress in one state, Pennsylvania, continuing to grow (Bean, Dole, Nelson, Belcastro, & Zigmond, 2015).

In the end, though, the government refused to drink from the glass entirely and cut its funding. Bush was vulnerable and too tempting a political target, and an aggrieved reading establishment was likely glad to see it go. Despite its popularity among its participants, there was little pushback from them or the public at large. The scandal had tainted the largest project of its kind, perhaps ever, and a project that could claim some success.

In addition to the taint of scandal, the general lack of pushback about the defunding of RF may have also been due to a general sense of weariness when it came to the ongoing reading wars. What remained was a tenuous cease-fire: the rise of "balanced literacy" as a potential middle ground. However, as Seidenberg (2014) has pointed out, "fashioning a coherent pedagogy out of opposing views is more challenging than the injunction to use the best of both" (p. 280).

Not surprisingly, as of this writing, the reading wars appear to be heating up again, with those advocating for systematic explicit instruction now working together under the banner of the "science of reading" (Seidenberg,

Borkenhagen & Kearns, 2020). In chapter 6, we consider in more depth the potential ways to attain a much-needed middle-ground position.

SUMMARY

The publication of *A Nation at Risk* in 1983 marked the beginning of what was to become a four-decade effort to reform our public schools that continues to this day. Efforts to reform reading in particular gathered steam during this period, with the pendulum swinging between code and comprehension-based approaches.

First, there was a token increase in phonics in commercial readers accompanied by increased use of phonics worksheets that were largely ineffective and the subject of considerable criticism. Partly in reaction to the phonics instruction at the time, as well as a wave of reading research in the related fields of psychology, sociology, linguistics, and psycholinguistics, the 1980s and 1990s saw the rise (and eventual fall) of whole language, a naturalistic method of teaching reading that stressed teacher autonomy over more prescriptive types of instruction.

The whole language era was followed by a flurry of state and federal reading policy initiatives culminating in the *NRP*, the product of a panel of experts commissioned by Congress to make explicit "scientifically based" recommendations about reading instruction to classroom teachers. The *NRP* provided the impetus for the largest federally sponsored reading experiment in history: Reading First (RF) part of the NCLB Act of 2001.

RF was designed to support teachers as they employed teaching practices referred to as "scientifically based," that is, consistent with the findings of the *NRP*. RF ultimately fell victim to a political scandal and mixed results leading to the present: a continued search for middle ground midst the reemergence of the reading wars.

Bill's entry into higher education as an Assistant Professor of Special Education coincided with the publication of *A Nation at Risk* and his career in higher education was buffeted by the waves of reading reform just described. In chapter 5, Bill tells of his struggles as a teacher educator to ensure his students were prepared to teach students with special needs to read. Also described is Bill's experience designing and implementing Project PRIDE, a multitiered reading system that Bill had hoped would transcend the politics of reading by basing instruction on student performance, not philosophy.

Chapter 5

Experiences

A Thirty-Year Career in Teacher Education, 1983–2013

Bursuck received his Ph.D. in special education from the University of Illinois at Urbana-Champaign in 1982 and began a career in higher education—teacher education that spanned four decades. During that time he prepared general and special education teachers at both the preservice and in-service levels to teach reading and other academic skills to students with special needs. His work culminated in attaining the dream of a lifetime: being awarded a federal model demonstration grant to implement a multitier system of reading instruction with struggling readers in three urban schools.

HIGHER EDUCATION/TEACHER EDUCATION

Bill began his graduate work at the University of Illinois the same year Edmonds published his work on effective schools. Bill had learned much in Vermont about how to teach reading to students with special needs but was in search of ways to better prepare teachers and schools to carry them out. When he arrived in the cornfields of central Illinois, the first thing he learned was that the professor with whom he was to study reading had, unbeknownst to him, left for another university.

The departure of Bill's advisor led to putting his interest in reading on hold. The culture at the University of Illinois emphasized writing, research, and grant procurement, and Bill was so caught up in the newness and excitement of being in a higher education environment that teacher preparation ceased being a priority as well.

Bill's work in reading did re-emerge, albeit indirectly, in his dissertation research, which was designed and carried out in the third year of his doctoral work. The literature at the time was showing that students with LD included in general education classes were more likely to be rejected by their peers than students without disabilities. However, previous studies had failed to take achievement into account when making their comparisons.

Bill's dissertation hypothesis was that it was achievement in general, and reading achievement specifically, that accounted for these differences in social acceptance. At the time, this hypothesis was part of a larger argument taking place within the special education community as to whether an LD was an actual disability or just low achievement—an argument that exists in some quarters to this day (Elliott, 2020).

Behaviorally oriented special educators such as Bill were dyslexia agnostics or even deniers. Given the lack of research verifying an organic cause for LD, they weren't ready to conclude that it existed, preferring to explain even severe reading deficits as due to inappropriate instruction. As mentioned earlier, Bill and his colleagues would often mockingly refer to the cause of LD as dyspedagogia.

Since then, several decades of research have provided convincing preliminary evidence for a biological basis for reading disabilities (Shaywitz, Morris, & Shaywitz, 2008), spawning as of this writing a research-based dyslexia screening device and policies requiring its use in more than twenty states (Johnston, 2019). Nonetheless, while it is certainly helpful for persons who have LD to know that they have an actual physical condition, and are not just lazy and dumb, effective interventions continue to be exclusively instructional rather than medical in nature, and more often than not they involve reading.

HIGHER EDUCATION 101 (AND THEN SOME)

In 1980, Bill took a visiting professorship at Penn State. He was given a three-course load on the quarter system, and all three classes were scheduled back-to-back, with the middle class located on the other side of campus! Weekdays were spent planning for, teaching, and recovering from these classes, while also being "daddy" for his two children. On weekends he would try to find nonfamily time to write up the results of his dissertation. Of course, Sunday evenings were spent planning for classes on Monday. It's a good thing he was young and had a supportive wife!

While at Penn State, Bill learned once again that the central mission of flagship universities' special education departments was primarily research, not teacher preparation. Penn State did have a sizeable teacher preparation program in special education, but at least to Bill, teacher preparation didn't seem to be a department priority. Of benefit to Bill was that he was given complete academic freedom. He could teach his methods class in any way he chose. For him, that was using the *Direct Instruction Reading* text (Carnine, Silbert, Kame'enui,

Slocum, & Travers, 2017), which stressed principles of designing reading instruction for students who were hard to teach. The principles were derived from the DISTAR programs but treated more generically in the text.

The text covered all aspects of reading that twenty years later were to become the "big five" of National Panel Report fame, namely, phonemic awareness, phonics, fluency, vocabulary, and comprehension. At the time, with whole language being on the rise, reading methods books covering phonemic awareness and phonics in anything but a cursory fashion were difficult if not impossible to find. Bill's goal was to give his students the tools to adapt whatever reading program they encountered when they became teachers, which was precisely what he had been unable to accomplish when he was a beginning teacher in Buffalo.

At the conclusion of each chapter were carefully designed activities requiring students to apply what they had learned in the chapter. For example, in the chapter on introducing and teaching letter sounds, students were required to demonstrate their understanding of systematic instruction by critiquing the sequence used by a hypothetical reading program and adapt it to make it more accessible for students with special needs. Of course, grading these application activities took a considerable amount of time—time that Bill could have spent furthering his research agenda. Still, he felt it was important to give his students information he had needed so badly as a beginning teacher.

Bill was eventually turned down for a tenure-track position largely because of his publication record, or lack of it. He had learned a key "publish or perish" lesson in what a former colleague had called "Higher Ed 101." This was a lesson that was to guide his future work as a college professor. Looking back, though, he couldn't honestly say that such a course of action was always for the betterment of preparing teachers.

Following his year at Penn State, Bill was fortunate to obtain a tenure-track position as an assistant professor at Northern Illinois University (NIU). NIU was a regional university, and in Illinois, as in many states, regional universities were responsible for the bulk of the teacher preparation, often having large undergraduate teacher preparation programs. The larger flagship land-grant schools tended to have smaller teacher preparation programs and emphasized research. However, NIU was different. While NIU did have sizeable teacher preparation programs at both the bachelor's and master's levels, NIU's special education faculty was highly regarded nationwide for its scholarship and grant writing accomplishments.

NIU's national standing was due to the efforts of a controversial department chair, long gone by the time Bill arrived, who was able to attract bright ambitious young faculty interested primarily in scholarship. A colleague and mentor of Bill's who came to the department during that time recounted that upon being hired he was told by the chair to be careful not to get too high student evaluations, the idea being that it would be a sign of neglect for scholarship.

It is difficult to imagine anyone saying this today when the public is at long last paying attention to what occurs in schools that prepare our nation's teachers. That said, the chair did build a department with a national reputation for obtaining grant money and publishing, an emphasis from which Bill was to benefit greatly.

THE NATION'S AT RISK, BUT WHERE'S THE URGENCY?

While faculty at NIU taught classes in undergraduate and graduate teacher preparatory programs, and several faculty had received federal grants to prepare special educators in areas of high need, teacher preparation was not a priority. The priority was scholarship, including grant writing. Undergraduate advisement was assigned to a nun who was a former special education teacher and school principal. The clinicals were directed by a former special education teacher and supervised by adjuncts.

Except for the teacher preparation grants at the master's level, the alignment between faculty classes and advisement and clinicals was minimal, as faculty were more involved in their own individual projects. As a result, students frequently took classes out of sequence and there was little relationship between methods classes and the clinical experiences.

The reading methods classes were in the general education department, and geared to typical child development, which, at that time, meant a whole language emphasis. In retrospect, and sadly, this seems much like descriptions of teacher education programs published today. The *Nation at Risk Report* was published during this time, and while faculty were supportive of it, it seemed to have little bearing on the day-to-day operation of the teacher education programs.

Bill's department eventually hired Diane Kinder, a colleague from the University of Oregon who was a master teacher. Diane had internalized Siegfried Engelmann's instructional design principles to the extent that, in Bill's view, like her mentor, it seemed that she could teach anybody anything. Working together to solve the scope and sequence problem, Bill and Diane designated three classes for an academic methods core, with each class stressing one of the core areas of reading, written language, and math.

Program coherence was achieved by adopting a DI approach in each of the classes, using texts consistent with that method. To address the disconnect between methods classes and clinicals, the methods "block" was instituted. In this arrangement, students took math and written language methods during the first ten weeks of the semester, and then participated in a six-week clinical designed to give them experience applying what they had learned in the two methods classes. While the classroom teaching in the block didn't exactly conform to the content covered in the class, the teachers at least allowed students to carry out the projects as prescribed in the methods courses.

Unfortunately, the block didn't include Bill's reading class. The relationship of that class to student teaching remained somewhat tenuous until years later when Bill began to place students who had taken his reading class with teachers who had been prepared to teach reading through his federal model demonstration grant. Bill felt this was the first and only time in his career in teacher education reading methods classes and student teaching were carefully and successfully aligned. Sadly, Bill's experiences aren't unique, either for general or special education teacher preparation. Nor are they history; indeed, many of the same problems exist today (Hindman, Morrison, Connor & Connor, 2020).

In retrospect, it is a fair question to ask why Bill didn't do more over the course of his career to directly improve teacher preparation. Part of the problem was that there were factors beyond faculty control, such as a lack of expertise of teachers in field settings as well as an unwieldy number of trainees. It is also a fact that the effort required would have interfered with Bill's writing and research. Bill had learned a hard lesson at Penn State. There was only so much time in a day. Unfortunately, until faculty professional goals and rewards are better aligned with teacher preparation, the situation will remain the same.

There is hope that in the current climate, when teacher education programs are being held more accountable by the public, teacher preparation will become *the* priority for most higher educators in education. Of course, there will always be a need for high-quality research, but that could be handled by a solid core of research institutions, for whom research would remain the central mission. Such research would need to be carefully coordinated with more field-oriented colleges and universities as well as public school teachers and administrators. Finally, there is nothing to prevent higher educators from pursuing research agendas directly related to teacher preparation, a much-needed research path(Hindman et al, 2020).

"THANK YOU AND GOD BLESS YOU" WORKSHOPS

Early in Bill's career, he and his colleagues were frequently contracted to conduct professional development workshops with surrounding school districts. IDEA had been in effect a relatively short time and school districts were looking for help implementing its regulations. At first, most of these professional development activities consisted of what were later characterized as "Thank You and God Bless You" workshops. In these sessions, the workshop leader stood and delivered. Teachers were left to carry out what was recommended on their own, with little follow-up guidance.

Bill approached these workshops conscientiously, always preparing carefully, and making a considerable effort to make them practical. After all, he had experienced firsthand in Buffalo the difference between helpful and irrelevant professional development. Besides, teachers were a tough, skeptical audience, as they were the ones left with the responsibility for carrying out practices that Bill and colleagues had often done in different contexts or, sometimes, not even at all.

Yet, in the back of their minds they all knew this type of professional development was ineffective. Bill and his colleagues performed it anyway, because they were expected to do it, but also because of the pay. They would often refer to these workshops sarcastically as prostitution: essentially, selling their bodies for money.

Bill's first experience delivering what he perceived to be effective professional development came during his second year at NIU. Bill had been interested in curriculum-based assessment (CBA) as a necessary complement to standardized testing since Vermont, where he had experimented with minimum objectives systems in his role as a CT. From that experience, Bill learned that when teachers were involved in selecting and testing the skills they covered in class, they were more likely to directly teach them.

Providing such a focus was particularly important in reading, where teachers could easily become distracted by the many different skills and activities covered in their core basal reading series. Reductionism, while always controversial in general education circles, has its place, as long as teachers don't lose sight of the big picture.

CBA solved another problem revealed by special education researchers at the time. Standardized tests often do not align with what teachers are teaching, making them of little help teaching and monitoring student progress. By testing skills not directly taught, standardized tests can favor students who have been exposed to content in other settings while depressing the performance of students of limited experiences, for whom incidental learning is less likely.

In conjunction with a local special education cooperative, Bill and a colleague, Elliott Lessen, developed CBAID (curriculum-based assessment and instructional design). The idea was to screen and monitor student progress in reading and math using informal assessments that were developed collaboratively with the teachers based on what the teachers were actually teaching. In this way, the assessments represented a more direct match with the curriculum than traditional standardized achievement tests. CBAs could also be given more frequently, lending themselves to more closely monitoring the progress of individual students who may be at risk or have disabilities.

CBAID foreshadowed Bill's later work in reading using a multitiered model that depended on curriculum-based measures to assign students to tiers and monitor their progress. The method of professional development used in CBAID was a definite improvement over the "Thank You and God Bless You" workshops described earlier. CBAID was a long-term project, carried out in careful conjunction with a large special education cooperative. CBAID training was intensive, with teacher feedback and support provided on-site on an ongoing basis. In this way, teachers were carefully prepared to construct and interpret all of the assessments, making for a successful project.

Bill was also able to publish the results of the project in a leading special education journal, enabling him to satisfy his obligations to both effective teacher preparation and his pursuit of tenure through scholarship. Thus was practiced a process referred to earlier that appears well suited for higher education, teacher preparation in the current climate where "publish and perish" has clashed with increasing levels of accountability within the ranks of teacher educators.

BUILDINGS AND WORLDS APART

Special education at NIU did not comprise its own department. Before a department reorganization in 2000, it was part of a mega-department consisting of educational psychology and counseling. General education teacher preparation had its own department within which reading, later to be referred to by the broader term literacy, was an area of emphasis. Special education and reading faculty were separated both physically and philosophically.

The tradition in most special education teacher preparatory programs in the 1980s was to assign the teaching of reading methods to the reading faculty. After all, reading faculty were trained in just that, while at that time special educators were trained to be learning specialists, receiving preparation that was more general in nature. Today, it is difficult to read the *Chronicle of Higher Education* and not find jobs earmarked special education literacy, an indication that, at least as perceived by special educators, the general education approach to teaching reading to students with disabilities is not meeting their needs. Then, that was not the case. Jobs in special education tended to be delineated based on disability (i.e., mild or severe, LD, BD, intellectual disabilities) or level of teaching (elementary or secondary).

When Bill began at NIU, methods classes in special education stressed general principles of learning rather than the teaching of subject-matter content per se. The assumption was that once teachers knew and understood the teaching-learning process, they would be able to teach any skill or content area. Special educators saw themselves as learning specialists. Concerning reading, the emphasis was on how to design effective instruction in general, with less direct emphasis placed on specific subject-matter areas such as reading.

The practice of preparing generalists while leaving preparation for teaching reading up to reading faculty began to change through the 1980s and 1990s. Reading faculty had always been oriented toward approaches emphasizing comprehension coupled with whole word memorization approaches to word identification. The advent of whole language ideas at the time allowed even less room for systematic, explicit skill instruction, which an ever-increasing research base was showing necessary for students who were at risk or who had LD. Not surprisingly, student teachers in special education frequently complained that they were unprepared for teaching their students with disabilities to read and that the approach taken in their reading classes wasn't structured enough.

While to the casual outsider, the obvious solution would have been for Bill and his colleagues to collaborate with their reading colleagues to work out a plan to better meet the needs of teacher candidates in both general and special education, such an initiative was rarely if ever undertaken, at least at NIU. The philosophical divide between the two areas was already so wide that it was easier to complain about the reading classes amongst ourselves and then create or modify our own courses to ensure that our students acquired the needed expertise.

It was also the case that collaboration with reading colleagues was simply not a priority. In retrospect, the time spent would have benefited both sides of the reading divide. The literacy program needed an approach to teaching word identification that was more structured for struggling readers, whose numbers were fast becoming a national issue. Programs in special education needed a more comprehensive approach to teaching reading as well, one that emphasized the careful teaching of vocabulary and comprehension as well as word identification.

The bottom line was that perceived "drill and kill" met perceived "hit and miss" and never the twain did meet. Special education faculty conducted reading methods one way and the literacy faculty the other way. It was then left to the students to sort out what to do in student teaching settings where the quality of literacy instruction was mixed at best.

Schools of education have a long history of being criticized for lacking the knowledge base required to be considered a true discipline. While the relationship between teacher preparation and student reading outcomes is complicated, schools of education have not been immune from criticism in these days of teacher accountability. Bill's experiences during these years as a teacher educator show that some criticism may be justified, especially as it relates to reading instruction.

RIDING THE PENDULUM

Chapter 4 described the period of the 1980s through the mid-1990s when the rapid rise of the whole language philosophy dominated reading instruction both in public schools and in higher education, teacher education programs. Bill was dismayed at the continuing reading wars narrative, having experienced nearly two decades of phonics being maligned or at best ignored by his higher education colleagues in general education.

Bill's students were continually misinformed that the English language was too irregular for phonics to be effective and that students taught phonics would not enjoy reading and/or become readers who would be "word callers," reading text accurately, but without understanding. The divergence in reading philosophies between general and special education teacher educators eventually led to Bill's special education colleagues offering their own reading class. This class would be the only direct exposure special education majors would get teaching beginning and advanced phonics skills systematically and explicitly.

There was the additional concern that future general education teachers would also be unprepared to teach students with special needs to read at a time when there was an increasing emphasis on including students with disabilities in general education classes. Teacher candidates in general education were required to take one class on inclusive practices, though there was hardly room within one course to provide the in-depth reading content they needed.

Bill was encouraged by research findings showing that not all children required the same instruction in order to learn to read (Snow, Burns, & Griffin, 1998). For years, many educators had been saying, "all children learn differently." In truth, Bill found such statements frustrating, feeling that DI, if properly carried out, could benefit most if not all students, disabled or not. Nonetheless, thirty years had elapsed since research from Project Follow Through and numerous other studies had shown DI to be effective. Yet, except for pockets of exceptions here and there, educators had chosen to ignore this method of teaching.

Research showed that as many as 30–35 percent of children learned to read quite naturally and that the remaining students required varying degrees of additional intensity in order to become fluent readers. Children at risk due to poverty, disability, or a native language difference needed the most careful reading instruction. To Bill, this finding provided a possible political opening. Why not cede the "natural" readers to the "literacy" folks and provide more systematic explicit instruction to the remainder?

Bill entered into collaborative discussions about developing a model of prevention-based early reading instruction with Shirley Dickson, a colleague who had been involved in using multiple instructional tiers as an innovative way of delivering reading instruction. Multitiered instruction employs the systematic use of increasingly intensive "research-based" interventions, with a level of intensity determined by students' response to instruction on reading performance assessments. This multitier approach, known as Response to Intervention (RTI), was recommended in the 2004 IDEA as an alternative way to identify students with LD. When a multitier approach is part of a school-wide system of instruction, it is referred to as Multitier Systems of Support (MTSS).

Multitier approaches are based on the assumption that approximately 75–90 percent of students can learn to read given high quality instruction in a research-based, core reading program or Tier 1. Approximately 10–25 percent of students may require more moderately intensive reading instruction in Tier 2. The remaining 2–10 percent require highly intensive instruction and possible special education in Tier 3 (Fletcher, Lyon, Fuchs, & Barnes, 2019). In some systems, special education comprises an additional tier.

With a multitier approach, the big five of reading—phonemic awareness, phonics, fluency, vocabulary, and comprehension—could potentially be delivered as systematically and explicitly as needed based on the needs of each student, not the philosophical orientation of the teacher. Students who learn to read more naturally could do so in Tier 1, receiving the least intensive reading instruction in the school district's core classroom reading program. Students who require more support to become fluent readers receive more intensive instruction in tiers that provide more carefully designed instruction. Bill felt that in this way the either-or, one-size-fits-all mentality of the reading wars could be avoided, a win-win, or at least that is what he thought would happen.

A key part of a multitier model is having an assessment instrument that can accurately assign students to the appropriate tiers. Bill attended a presentation by Mark Shinn and Roland Good, then both at the University of Oregon, about a curriculum-based measure they had developed to help teachers screen students early for potential reading problems and then continually monitor their progress. The measure was called Dynamic Indicators of Basic Early Literacy Skills (DIBELS). As mentioned earlier, Bill and his colleagues had long been a supporter of using informal, CBAs to monitor student progress.

Shinn and Good presented research to show the importance of intervening early with struggling readers, and how what they called curriculum-based measurement (CBM) could be used to continually monitor their progress. DIBELS became a critical part of Bill's multitier model, ensuring that students were placed in tiers that met their needs.

Bill's years in the public schools as both a general and special educator taught him that teacher educators need a firm grasp of the realities of classroom teaching. Perhaps that was why he always held professors who spent time in actual classrooms in the greatest regard. Anita Archer was at the top of that list of professors who, in Bill's view, escaped the confines of the ivory tower. Archer's professional development with teachers often involved teaching model lessons on a range of classroom levels and subjects with only the night before her workshops to prepare in her hotel room. Even with that short timetable, she was able to develop engaging, effective lessons!

Bill viewed Archer as the ultimate "teachers' teacher." With her success in mind, early in his career at NIU, Bill tutored a boy in reading at a school in rural Illinois and found that being able to refer to this experience in his college reading methods class benefited his special education majors. Later, Bill was to spend a good part of a sabbatical leave teaching a student for whom even Tier 3 interventions were ineffective. When Bill became interested in multitiered reading instruction, he decided to first develop and pilot the program in an actual school.

At the time, Bill's wife Beth taught special education in a rural school in northern Illinois. Her principal was a former principal at a famous school for students with LD in the Chicago area called the Cove School. Bill felt her principal would be receptive to developing a school-wide multitiered reading program using the DIBELS as its major assessment component.

The school was already using a language-based reading program, *Wilson Language*, that Bill knew would be compatible with the systematic, explicit approach taken in his and Shirley's program. Bill scheduled a meeting with the principal to describe the proposed program. He and Shirley said they would work free of charge if she would allow us to develop and pilot our program in her school. The principal consented, and so began what would become a ten-year journey into multitier reading.

Bill's work with the multitier model occurred at a time when whole language had just fallen from grace, and the popularity of phonics instruction was re-emerging. While the time was certainly ripe for programs that included systematic, explicit phonics, it was never his intent to ride another pendulum swing. In fact, several years later Bill would begin all of his presentations to teachers with a slide showing a pendulum with a red line drawn through it, and the caption "No More Pendulum."

Bill was a firm supporter of carefully taught vocabulary and comprehension instruction, but he felt that students needed to learn strategies to identify words accurately and fluently as well. As explained earlier, logic and politics demanded a *phonics as needed* approach. Those who could learn to read more naturally would get what they needed in the least intensive tier. The intent was to avoid ideology and teach based on student performance. Little did Bill realize that the very act of assessing discrete reading skills itself would be viewed negatively by the literacy establishment. Indeed, the DIBELS assessment became controversial due to its prominent role in RF, with an entire book written on its limitations and misuse (Goodman, 2006).

A discussion about the pros and cons of DIBELS is beyond the scope of this book. However, the fact that it has been viewed so harshly by its critics is not (Goodman, 2006). The presence of vitriolic criticisms of DIBELS and instruments like it is a sign of the continuing reading wars, preventing, in Bill's view, a potentially more productive dialogue.

That dialogue could include a discussion of when its use is helpful, potential misuses and their prevention, and how the technical quality of DIBELS could be improved. Still, at the time, with decades of reading research to support systematic, explicit reading instruction, if not yet his and Shirley's multitier system of delivery, they felt the wind at their backs and were supremely confident they would get results.

PROJECT PRIDE

Following the first year of program development, Shirley and Bill applied and received a federal Eisenhower training grant to prepare their teachers to implement multitier instruction school-wide in grades K-3. The results of that effort were modest yet encouraging. Bill and Shirley were motivated by the logic of the model, the strong case for systematic, explicit instruction in the research literature, and the pent-up demand resulting from two decades of phonics being out of favor.

They applied for and were granted federal money from the Office of Special Education Research (OSERS) to implement their model in three urban schools in a medium-sized city in the upper Midwest. Thus was born Project PRIDE, a model demonstration grant to provide multitier reading instruction.

Project PRIDE represented a return to urban education, the setting where Bill had started his teaching career forty years earlier. The goal of the project was to increase reading achievement in all three of its urban schools. A common theme in special education throughout Bill's nearly five decades in that field was that deficiencies in general education reading programs inflated the number of students identified as having reading disabilities. Thus, the project had the additional goal of reducing the number of students receiving special education in reading.

While the pilot work for PRIDE had been in a rural school, direct systematic instruction was a key part of the model and had shown to be quite effective with children in urban and low-income areas. What was most disturbing to Bill about his return to urban education was the realization of how little things had changed. Classrooms looked the same; teachers of color were still in the minority; basal readers still dominated; and while new "leveled books" were now present in each class, most students were unable to read the ones at their grade level.

The big difference was that now Bill felt he had the know-how to make a difference. Bill saw PRIDE as the "work of his life." He felt strongly that everything he had done professionally up until that time had led him there, and that, unlike in Buffalo, this time he would be successful.

Bill and his university colleagues used to say that while getting a grant-funded was exhilarating, the problem was that you eventually had to do what you proposed. One immediate problem for Project PRIDE was that Shirley, the Co-principal Investigator, left for Texas to coordinate a statewide reading effort. Fortunately, Bill was able to hire Mary Damer, a former school principal and supervisor at NIU as a full-time project director. She and Bill were on the same page philosophically, both of them being strong advocates for systematic, explicit phonics as part of a total reading program. Bill and Mary were both firmly committed to the principles of instruction as delineated in the DI programs.

As full-scale school reform is about to conclude its fourth decade, one clear finding that has emerged is that change does not come easily (Payne, 2008). One problem is that teachers may not define success in the same way. Project staff may emphasize test scores as reflecting growth while teachers may view life skills as more important, believing that testing doesn't reflect actual student learning. Also, years of repeated failure may create an ideology of failure that teachers believe in more strongly than any solution. Schools may also be so demoralized that change has to depend on pressure being provided.

While all of these factors were in play in the Project PRIDE implementation, several program features lessened their impact. Bill and his Project Director Mary had the strong support of principals, who were capable of applying pressure and expecting more from teachers when needed. All three principals supported the DIBELS assessments, which helped provide the project with a focus and agreed-upon, measurable goals. However, while administrative leverage was necessary, it was not sufficient. Over the three years of the project, Bill and Mary were able to conduct PRIDE effectively by providing ongoing, relevant support for staff. Ultimately, they were able to deliver tangible results in the form of improved student reading scores.

DI was an important part though not the only instructional component of Project PRIDE. Yet its overall dedication to the design of instruction was evidenced in every aspect of the project. DI's supporters are known for having such confidence in the design of their programs that a failure to achieve success is seen as a failure to implement correctly. DI teachers never blame the children, their home life, poverty, or learning challenges for failure to achieve. Thus, from the very beginning, carrying out Project PRIDE as designed was too important to be left to chance.

It has been said that there is a tendency among some educators to emphasize pedagogy to the point of fetishizing it (Payne, 2008). Well, if that is the case, then Mary and Bill were full-fledged DI fetishizers! Recall Bill's early experience with DI recounted in chapter 3. After six years of urban teaching characterized by instruction that was well intended, but hit and miss, and ultimately ineffective, he was relieved to find an approach that was logical and designed with such care that carrying it out correctly actually mattered. Success, defined as catching struggling students up to grade level, was a matter of getting administrators to support this approach and teachers to carry it out a faithfully-no easy task.

The project management plan called for a gradual, staggered implementation, beginning in kindergarten during the first year, with one additional grade added each year so that by the fourth year, the model would be carried out throughout K-3 in all three project schools. Bill felt such an implementation timeline was realistic given the fact that only Mary was full-time in the schools and there was no one in any of the three schools with the expertise to provide needed support to the teachers alone. Bill and Mary were to learn years later the importance of having enough staff to provide adequate support when attempting, unsuccessfully, to bring PRIDE to scale.

In the multitier program, Tier 1, the schools' core reading program, was considered the crucial first line of prevention. The goal of Tier 1 was to meet the needs of at least 80 percent of the students. The school district had invested in the *Harcourt* and *Open Court* reading programs as their district-wide reading programs.

Because of RF and the desire to sell to schools participating in that project, the *Harcourt* and *Open Court* reading programs had been revised to emphasize more systematic explicit instruction, including in phonics, than most of the other reading programs available at the time. Tier 2 comprised extra small-group practice on skills covered in Tier 1, and Tier 3 was a commercial DI program called *Reading Mastery* (*RM*), which was thoroughly systematic, explicit, and scripted.

Bill and Mary felt the Tier 1 goal of 80 percent of students meeting the benchmark using *Harcourt* and *Open Court* as designed was achievable in middle and upper-income schools. However, PRIDE schools had a high percentage of low SES learners who were not meeting benchmarks on the state high-stakes reading test. Bill and Mary thought these students needed instruction that was even more efficient, systematic, and explicit. Also, years of layering one educational trend after another had created teachers' guides that were sprawling and unwieldy, and *Harcourt* and *Open Court* were no exception.

To make *Harcourt* and *Open Court* more instructionally potent and accessible, Mary and Bill scaffolded the lessons for teachers by developing lesson enhancements. The enhancements were features of DI incorporated into each lesson. They were developed by constructing lesson outlines that identified which skills were essential to cover, corresponding teaching examples, and semi-scripted guidelines for teaching them.

Professional development in PRIDE consisted of two major areas: making data-based decisions using DIBELS and delivering accurately the *Harcourt* or *Open Court* lesson adaptations. Each summer Mary and Bill held an intensive week-long training session for teachers in the incoming grade level. The workshop was followed by monthly follow-up workshops, but, most importantly, ongoing, on-site classroom coaching during the school year by Mary.

Mary spent more time coaching in classrooms where DIBELS assessments showed that students weren't gaining needed reading skills at an acceptable rate. She practiced the scripts with teachers and modeled by teaching their classes when the scripts weren't taught accurately. Mary also helped teachers understand and appreciate gains in the DIBELS test data, honoring staff by celebrating their successes. In essence, she employed coaching strategies that have since been verified by research (Coburn & Waulfin, 2012) as helping teachers better teach struggling learners to read.

A key goal that first year was convincing teachers at the three project schools that teaching using the PRIDE model would lead to higher rates of success for all students. The difficulty of implementing these changes became clear during an early visit to one of the project schools to explain how the model was to be carried out. This school was selected due to the low percentage of its students meeting standards on the state's high-stakes reading test (31 percent). Midway through this introductory presentation, which was greeted with a combination of silence and barely concealed hostility, the principal rose and said, "If our reading scores weren't in the toilet, these people wouldn't be here in the first place."

The teachers hadn't chosen to participate in PRIDE, but their principal had, bringing to mind the rejoinder that change rarely comes due to exclusively voluntary means alone (Payne, 2008). In the course of four years, Bill and Mary made solid progress in all three schools, even though the teachers had not chosen the model voluntarily. When one teacher who had been the most resistant during training observed her students reading at far higher levels than they had in previous years, she tearfully apologized, sadly recalling students in previous classes who hadn't learned to read and saying that she felt she had failed them. Another first grade teacher who was about to retire said that she thought of the PRIDE years as the "Camelot" of her teaching career.

Bill and Mary felt strongly that they shouldn't be asking the teachers to do anything they couldn't do themselves. When student teachers teaching Tier 2 and 3 groups left for their college breaks, Bill and Mary taught their groups. Taking over the classes enhanced their credibility by showing they were able to do what they were telling the teachers to do.

Teaching during intersessions also clearly demonstrated the importance of academic press, sending a clear message that the amount of time spent teaching was important and that students could ill afford missing instruction. Bill and Mary created a sense of urgency around reading instruction, a level of urgency so missing in many of Bill's previous experiences. A lack of student achievement just wasn't acceptable.

At the same time, Bill and Mary provided teachers with all of the support they needed, feeling morally bound to require accountability on both sides of the equation. Teachers expressed their surprise that either Bill or Mary (mostly Mary) was in the schools every day after the initial training. The teachers were accustomed to the "Thank You and God Bless You" workshops described earlier whereby consultants conducted one or two days of training comprising telling them what to change, and then never seeing them again.

At the conclusion of the project, Bill surveyed teachers as to whether they thought their school should continue to implement PRIDE the following year. Twenty-nine or 85 percent of the teachers responded. Of the twenty-nine who responded, twenty-eight or 97 percent wanted the project to continue.

The project city had lost a desegregation lawsuit in the early 1990s. One of the key issues in that suit involved the tracking of minority children. Grouping children by ability level can be problematic for students of color if it is done inappropriately. Tracking has a long history of lowered student expectations reflected in watered-down curricula taught by poorly prepared teachers, conditions that remain in play today as our nation continues to struggle to narrow the achievement gap between the rich and poor students.

In contrast, grouping can be effective if done appropriately. Bill believed that there was a sweet spot regarding how and how not to group, and that Project PRIDE's multitier, data-based decision-making, high curricular expectations, use of evidence-based reading practices, and intensive teacher supports were those sweet spots.

In the end, in the most successful PRIDE school, 68 percent of the children were meeting standards on the highly challenging high-stakes state test, up from 31 percent of the students when the project started. The increases at the other two schools were more modest: an increase of 14 percent of students meeting standards (from forty-one to fifty-five) at one school and 5 percent (from sixty-two to sixty-seven) at the other. The final school's data are somewhat misleading as it lost its magnet school status during the first year of the project, leading to an increase in students at risk as well as increased class size. To illustrate, during the 1999–2000 school year, the year prior to our project, 62 percent of this school's third graders met the reading standard; during the next year that number had decreased to 50 percent.

Also of note was that over the four years of the project, the total number of students in the three schools who were identified for special education had fallen, from forty-five to twenty-seven students. While not conclusive, a likely explanation was that the project was able to eliminate the need for special education for some students by providing them with a more intensive approach to teaching reading in Tiers 2 and 3.

As said before, Bill was sensitive to the criticism that systematic, explicit reading programs included a level of student practice thought by some to be detrimental to students; that is, "drill and kill." In his view, one way to improve student attitudes toward reading was to teach them to read better. After three years, the attitudes of all PRIDE students toward reading were assessed. The results showed that regardless of grade level, or whether they had easily acquired reading skills or needed intensive support, students uniformly expressed positive attitudes toward reading. That, combined with their achievement gains, meant that they were very much alive! After that, Bill replaced the "drill and kill" mantra with what he liked to call "drill and thrill!"

Ultimately, Project PRIDE, like RF to come, was not an experimental study. Thus, it is impossible to determine precisely what was responsible for student gains in the three PRIDE schools. Certainly having systematic, explicit reading programs in all five areas of reading—phonemic awareness, phonics, fluency, vocabulary, and comprehension—helped. However, strong principal and coaching support as well as a system of data decision-making using DIBELS were also important. Additional resources coupled with the focus and excitement that often accompanies a new approach likely also played a part.

Though less quantifiable, Bill and Mary witnessed a major change in school culture at their most successful school. The teachers and principal were proud of what they had accomplished and felt empowered to continue the project. One teacher commented that her students were able to read the trade books in her classroom for the first time—and this was a teacher who was one of the biggest skeptics at first. Several years later, worried by test scores indicating their students' reading scores were slipping, the school brought Bill and Mary back for a refresher course.

A potential problem with grouping students according to skill levels is that minority students can be overrepresented in the lower-performing groups, which in PRIDE were Tiers 2 and 3. Because the district had been the subject of a discrimination lawsuit related to grouping, the racial makeup of PRIDE's tier groupings was of special interest. Bill was relieved when the results showed that the Tier 2 and 3 groups were proportional to the number of white, Asian, and African American students in all three schools.

While their results showed that more children met state standards in reading as a result of Project PRIDE, too many students did not. The number of students who failed to meet standards ranged from 33 percent to 45 percent of all students, a disturbing finding. However, whether or not a student met the standard was determined by whether they met or exceeded a single cut-off score on the state test. The use of cut-off scores can obscure gains made by students who progressed but still hadn't made the cut-off.

It's also fair to say that change takes time. Given its staggered implementation, in the end, PRIDE had only been carried out school-wide for one year. Most experts agree that reform efforts need at least three years to get results, and that the most significant results occur between the third and fifth years (Payne, 2008).

Still, there were programmatic issues as well. Based on estimates from the field of mental health and existing multitier projects at the time, Bill had expected that roughly 15 percent of students would require a Tier 2 intervention, while 5 percent would need support in Tier 3, the most intensive tier. The results showed that significantly more students needed Tier 2 and 3 support, with 20 percent requiring Tier 2 and 30–35 percent requiring Tier 3.

One implication of this finding is that in schools with a high percentage of students at risk, Tier 1 may need to be more intensive. Bill's Tier 1 program was enhanced and carried out with a reasonable degree of fidelity, but even more intensity may have been needed in the form of additional instructional time, more carefully designed instruction, and smaller class sizes.

When Project PRIDE was in progress, Bill continued his duties as a professor of special education. As Bill related in chapter 3, perhaps the biggest problem in teacher education programs that he had experienced was the disconnect between university methods coursework and the clinical-student teaching sites. What could have been his most satisfying experience with Project PRIDE was the preparation his NIU student teachers received when student teaching in that program.

The teacher candidates in special education had learned all about systematic explicit reading instruction and multitiered reading in Bill's reading methods class, including the use of DIBELS as an assessment tool. As student teachers in PRIDE schools, they were able to better internalize their course content by seeing it in practice and then doing it. Never in all Bill's years as an education professor did he feel his students were receiving better preparation. Unfortunately, given that PRIDE only included three schools, Bill was able to accommodate only a few students each semester. Still, he learned that effective teacher education was possible if the right pieces were in place.

PRIDE GOETH BEFORE THE FALL

Bill and Mary always felt that if they could just show results, the school district would notice and begin to use their multitier model in other schools that had a high percentage of struggling readers. While the results of PRIDE were far from conclusive, they were promising, particularly at their most successful school. Bill and Mary felt that they had left a successful model to build upon.

In May of the final year of the project, the district hired a new superintendent. At the time, thirty of fifty-two of its schools were on the State Department of Education's categories of "warning," "watch," or "corrective action." However, instead of examining what might be working, and making changes in other schools based on actual results, a new superintendent and the literacy staff he brought with him to the district rigidly embraced "balanced literacy" and not DI, especially systematic, explicit phonics.

All too often, balanced literacy can be a code phrase for reducing the intensity of phonics instruction. When the principal at one of the PRIDE schools resisted changing back to more of a sight word, comprehension-based reading approach, she was transferred, but not before she was accused of cheating on the state tests, a charge for which she was eventually exonerated. The most successful PRIDE school was also discouraged from continuing the project, and their principal was eventually transferred as well. A recent Google search revealed the results of the 2017–2018 school report cards for the three PRIDE schools.

The report cards revealed that only 3 percent, 3 percent, and 12 percent of the students respectively were proficient in English-Language-Arts. Two schools were designated as underperforming. One school was designated as "lowest" performing, a school that "is in the lowest-performing 5 percent of schools" in the state. Even given the fact that these results were based on a more difficult Common Core assessment, it is clear that the gains had evaporated.

Bill was obviously discouraged by the dismissal of work he had considered successful but was proud of what he had accomplished. He still felt the PRIDE model had merit. During the final year of the project, Bill and Mary decided to write a reading methods text describing their methods. They hoped that the text would be used by teacher education programs that prepared elementary education general educators. They felt then, and do to this day, that systematic, explicit instruction should be *one* part of their repertoire. Unfortunately, the book has almost exclusively become a text used in special education teacher education programs. While not exactly a shooting war in those days, the reading wars were far from over.

CAROLINA ON MY MIND

In the summer of 2004, Bill moved to North Carolina where he was hired as a professor of Special Education at the University of North Carolina at Greensboro. Multitier reading and its related RTI was just beginning to catch on nationwide, at least in part because it was consistent with the recently passed NCLB Act and its RF grants.

During Bill's first year at UNCG, one of his original PRIDE principals contacted him. She had taken a job as an assistant superintendent for instruction in a large, diverse, low-income suburban district in the Southeastern United States. She contacted him to see if he would be interested in implementing a PRIDE-like system of reading instruction in her district. The district was already a participant in RF, the multibillion-dollar federal reading project described in chapter 3. The former principal had been pleased with PRIDE's approach and results and wanted Bill and Mary to do the same as part of their RF grant.

Bill was thrilled, as this was an opportunity to share the multitier model more broadly. He and Mary even started their own company in anticipation of this project as well as other possible projects to come. The company, registered in the state of North Carolina, was called Multitier LLC. Lost in the excitement of the moment, however, was that they didn't have the number of supportive personnel needed to bring the model to scale. Kindergarten through eighth grade teachers graduating from general education teacher preparatory programs typically do not receive training in phonics, DI, or systematic and explicit instruction in general.

Providing teachers with the support they needed to ensure program fidelity proved to be a daunting task requiring hours of training and coaching. Bill and Mary had assumed that the teachers' teacher education classes would have at least emphasized the teaching of comprehension and vocabulary, but teachers told them repeatedly that although their college professors talked about those areas of literacy, they often failed to demonstrate exactly what careful teaching in these areas looked like.

Bill's initiation to the school district was a Friday afternoon presentation to hundreds of teachers, whereby he introduced the multitier model. While Bill had given this talk many times, never was it before this large a group of teachers on a Friday afternoon. The district roped off the seats in the back to encourage teachers to sit as close as possible, but, in a sign of what was to come, many teachers jumped over the rope anyways.

Bill survived the initial presentation to teachers, but signs of problems to come were already in evidence. First and foremost, whereas he and Mary had three schools to support in their PRIDE sites, this district had forty elementary schools, most of which had 1,000 students, and the district wanted multitier reading carried out in all of them. Bill had just taken on a new job as a professor at UNCG, and there was no way for Mary to coach teachers in forty schools. It had been demanding enough adequately coaching at three schools in PRIDE. Bill and Mary tried to get the district to scale things back by insisting that fewer schools participate at first, but were unsuccessful.

Bill and Mary attempted to solve the problem of a lack of support staff by adopting a "train the trainer" model. Mary and three other district reading educators who knew the model prepared each school's reading coaches so they could in turn support their teachers. However, the backgrounds of the coaches differed, as did their need for support and enthusiasm toward the project. The schools that had RF grants had received training that paralleled Bill and Mary's. They could be more readily prepared to implement the reading program.

The schools that had never received RF training were starting from scratch. In the end, the quality of implementation was mixed. Some schools had knowledgeable coaches who supported the project and carried it out with higher fidelity. Unfortunately, many more did not.

The same dynamic was in evidence concerning the principals. With PRIDE, Bill and Mary were able to bring principals along gradually with weekly personal contact. This was impossible with forty large schools. Thus, as with the coaches, administrative support in the schools was inconsistent. Bill and Mary also encountered problems with upper district-level administrative turnover. The assistant superintendent responsible for hiring them left after a year and a half, followed a year later by the superintendent who had hired her. Their last year, during the district's opening school year staff program, the new superintendent had yelled out, "This year we are getting rid of those damned Yankee reading folks!"

Still, the principals who were seeing growth in their students' reading scores insisted that Bill and Mary stay the year and work with their schools. After that year, with a resistant superintendent and an implementation that was mixed in quality, the project ended. Once again, Bill and Mary had learned the hard lesson that when it came to school reform, having an effective model was not enough to bring about significant change.

REFLECTION

As Bill thought back about his career as a teacher educator, he couldn't help thinking how, ironically, it all started in the Teacher Corps, a Great Society, War on Poverty program that accepted him in large part because he had had no previous course work in teacher education. As Bill reflected upon his own work over almost half a century, he was reminded of the outcome of the work of the Holmes Group, a collection of teacher educators who formed a partnership in the mid-1980s not long after *A Nation At Risk* had been published.

The Holmes Group set the lofty goals of (1) changing the way teachers are educated; (2) helping bring about a true profession of teaching; (3) cooperating with school people in research that transforms the schools; and (4) restructuring teacher education departments to achieve these ends. After a decade of work, the effort was evaluated, and the title of the evaluation report is instructive: "The Rise and Stall of Teacher Education Reform." The report concluded that "the reform of professional education is so complicated and difficult that it has not yielded to any one reform group efforts to improve it" (cited in https://www1.udel.edu/holmes/origins.html).

Clearly, teacher education remained much the same during Bill's long tenure there, though it is a positive development that much more public attention is currently being paid to it. Whether this increased visibility and, with it, an increased level of accountability will ever produce enough effective teachers to bridge the achievement gap is unclear. In the meantime, the problems with teacher education that Bill encountered at the beginning of his career remain.

Seidenberg (2014) has written that teacher education in general and reading education in particular continue to lack an *agreed-upon* (1) scope and sequence of evidence-based teacher competencies, including those that involve teaching reading systematically and explicitly for those students who need it; (2) sequence of coursework that systematically and explicitly delivers those competencies and that is coordinated with classroom teachers employing these practices in schools; and (3) assessment system that accurately assesses whether teachers have acquired the identified competencies.

However elusive it may be, Bill was at least able to get a glimpse of the "promised land" when he placed student teachers in the three Project PRIDE schools, where their reading methods class and clinical settings came together seamlessly, creating reading educators whom he truly felt comfortable sending out to teach. Bill clings to the belief that attaining such a high level of teacher education on a larger scale, while daunting, is at least possible.

In retrospect, Bill's initial optimism about the political viability of multi-tiered systems of instruction appears to have been naive. He had envisioned a system that not only met a range of student reading needs but teaching philosophies as well. However, schools that are almost exclusively low SES, as his were, may be ill-suited for more naturalistic teaching strategies, even in Tier 1. A healthy majority of students at all three of the PRIDE schools were not meeting standards on state high-stakes tests, necessitating a more structured and prescriptive Tier 1.

It also appears that the reading establishment remains reluctant to cede control of any part of the reading infrastructure. Future efforts to seek agreement between the different parties involved in reading education need to be begun in earnest, a topic covered more thoroughly in chapter 6.

The fact that Bill and Mary were unable to bring Project PRIDE to scale was another disappointment. While this failure could at least in part be attributed to the fact that they were outsiders, both regionally and educationally, that is not the only explanation. They were outsiders when they began Project PRIDE as well but were able to overcome their outsider status by providing staff with the extensive technical and moral support they needed to enact the model with quality. The three PRIDE schools achieved measurable results, which proved to be sustaining for them, at least in the short run.

Support for teachers is key. In the larger district, Bill and Mary just didn't have the staff to provide the support needed to bring the model to scale. There were too many schools and too few trainers. The impact of this lack of staff and resources rings especially true because of recent research unearthing the difficulties involved when adopting a multitiered system (Gersten, Jayanthi, & Dimino, 2017), difficulties that have caused some scholars to even advocate for a model with fewer tiers (Fuchs & Fuchs, 2017).

Perhaps the most personally devastating outcome of Project PRIDE for Bill was the fact that the school district chose to ignore its success. The district actively worked to dismantle the multitier reading system at all three project schools soon after the PRIDE grant was concluded. In so doing, it also dismissed PRIDE as a potentially effective model for its many other failing schools—apparently based on ideology, not results.

From the time Bill was a consulting teacher in Vermont to his three decades in higher education, he had aspired to find a way to effectively teach struggling learners to read. He had also continued to believe, despite numerous examples to the contrary, that if it could just be shown that a given strategy worked, the powers that be would support its use. Not so, at least in this experience and with RF as well. It was at this point that the urge to write this book became so strong that it could not be denied.

Chapter 6

Policy and the Personal

What We Learned from Seven Decades of Reading Instruction and Reform

As the authors have discussed throughout this book, since the 1950s the United States has turned toward education and the teaching of reading as favored ways of addressing a variety of social, economic, and cultural issues. Toward reading in particular, in the last several decades various policies emerged that focused on reforming reading instruction and, it was hoped, improving students' academic and life outcomes. Educational policymakers and reformers have consistently sought to use reading instruction and reform as crucial weapons in the battle to end the American achievement gap.

Despite the enduring focus of the United States on reforming schools and reading instruction, studies suggest that this widescale, sustained attention on improvement has produced limited results. In a recent study, for instance, Hanushek, Peterson, Talpey, and Woessmann (2019) investigated student achievement since the 1960s. The authors asserted that

> the achievement gap between haves and have-nots in the U.S. remains as large as it was in 1966, when James Coleman wrote his landmark report and the nation launched a "war on poverty" that made compensatory education its centerpiece. That gap has not widened, as some have suggested. But neither has it closed. (p. 19)

These findings of the authors raise difficult questions: Is it good news that the achievement gap has remained static and not grown? Should we be disappointed at the lack of measurable progress toward closing the distance?

In the end, these are the questions that Americans have struggled with over the past several decades. In the 1950s, policymakers and public figures began championing a focus on reading reform as a means to combat illiteracy. The idea was that increased literacy would alleviate poverty and other ills and enable greater personal and group liberation. These same motivating factors remain today. In this book, the authors have described the effort to reform reading instruction and improve reading achievement in the United States over the last six decades. The authors have also discussed how and why those efforts have so often ended in disappointment.

A central issue throughout these times has been what Chall called "the great debate" regarding whether a phonics (sounding out) approach or the whole word, meaning-based (later in the form of "whole language" and "balanced literacy") approach to teaching reading worked best. As described in depth in chapters 1 and 2 of this book, this seemingly irresolvable, enduring tension has had profound effects on reading instruction, policies, and reform. These national trends left an indelible impact on millions of individual students, teachers, and educators. To help illuminate the effects of these policy and reform changes, the authors provided accounts of Bill Bursuck's experiences as a professional whose fifty-plus year career in education has been deeply involved in teaching, researching, and implementing reading methods.

Following a summary of the previous chapters, this chapter connects public history with personal experience by analyzing Bill's work in the context of broader themes of educational reform. In addition, the chapter presents lessons learned through the study and practice of reading instruction and reform. The chapter concludes by exploring whether a middle ground offers a possible, more hopeful approach to the future.

SUMMARY

In chapters 1–5, the authors condensed roughly seven decades of scholarship, policy, and practice related to the teaching of reading in our schools into two distinct periods: 1955–1983 and after 1983 to the present. The relevant professional experiences of Bill Bursuck during both of these periods were also described.

Policy before 1983

The publication of Flesch's *Why Johnny Can't Read* in 1955, followed by a series of research efforts in the 1960s, including Chall's landmark publication *Learning to Read: The Great Debate*, the First Grade Studies, and Project Follow Through largely brought an end to the look-say, Dick and Jane era of reading instruction that had dominated reading instruction in the first half of the twentieth century. All of these efforts recommended the inclusion of more systematic phonics in beginning reading instruction, though interpretations of the findings varied somewhat as to the relative importance of phonics as compared to other teaching and setting factors.

At least partly as a result of this divided interpretation, the integration of systematic, explicit phonics into the commercial readers of the day tended to be cosmetic in nature. While the First Grade Studies and Project Follow Through were supported with federal dollars, the primary federal effort during this period was the passage of Title 1 of the Elementary and Secondary Education Act of 1965, one of Lyndon Johnson's Great Society programs. Title 1, however, was mainly interested in leveling the playing field for disadvantaged learners by providing additional resources. How schools used those resources was generally left up to the states and individual schools.

During this period, Bill began his teaching career as both an elementary school teacher in an urban setting in Buffalo New York and then as a special education consulting teacher in rural Vermont. In Buffalo, Bill found his repertoire of reading strategies generally ineffective, causing him to seek out more knowledge through a federally sponsored master's degree program in special education and a position as a teacher consultant in the Vermont public schools. While in Vermont, Bill learned about a form of systematic, explicit instruction called DI. This approach to designing reading instruction was to be central to his future career as a scholar and teacher educator.

Policy after 1983

A Nation at Risk, a document published by the U.S. Department of Education in 1983, emphasized the importance of school achievement, including reading achievement, for the future economic well-being of our country, an idea that helped bring about an increased federal role in education over the three decades that followed.

The 1980s also gave rise to the whole language movement, an approach to fostering literacy that stressed naturalistic methods of reading instruction, often to the exclusion of systematic, explicit instruction in reading skills, including phonics. The decision-making framework within the whole language gave teacher judgment considerable sway as to how reading instruction was to be conducted.

In part in reaction to whole language, the 1990s saw the rise of bills coming out of state legislatures mandating the teaching of phonics in schools. A new federal focus on reading instruction followed, culminating in two initiatives: The *NRP* and RF, part of the NCLB Act of 2002.

The *NRP* was an attempt to provide teachers with a guide to reading instruction that was scientifically based. RF was a part of the NCLB Act of 2002 designed to reduce the achievement gap by applying the *NRP* findings in urban schools. RF was terminated in 2008 due to a political scandal and mixed results. The current status quo in reading appears to be shared by balanced literacy, an alleged code and meaning-based hybrid that has yet to be precisely defined or verified, and the 'science of reading,' the current holder of the phonics torch. And so the reading wars continue.

During this period, Bill entered the world of higher education teacher preparation in special education, with an emphasis on teaching reading in inclusive settings. As part of a special education teacher training program, Bill struggled to integrate content related to systematic, explicit reading instruction, including phonics, given that special education teacher candidates were taking their reading methods classes from a literacy faculty more oriented to whole language. He eventually taught his own reading class in order to ensure that his special education majors had the knowledge and skills to teach struggling readers.

Frustrated with the politics of reading, with a colleague, Bill developed a multitier reading program. The program emphasized systematic, explicit reading instruction in all areas, including phonics, but "as needed." The hope was that multitier programming would better accommodate a diversity of reading viewpoints.

Bill's work in multitier reading culminated in federal funding for a successful federal model demonstration grant, Project PRIDE. Project PRIDE was not continued by the school district after its funding expired, despite having had a positive impact on reading outcomes in its three urban schools. Soon after, Bill attempted to implement PRIDE to scale in a large, low SES suburban school district but failed largely due to the lack of resources.

ANALYSIS: UNDERSTANDING ONE EDUCATOR'S WORK WITHIN THE CONTEXT OF REFORM

In this section, the authors seek a deeper understanding of Bill's experiences recounted in chapters 3 and 5 by examining the key factors and enduring tensions present in school reform. The analysis is anchored in Craig Peck's (2017) summary of the history of urban school reform in the United States.

In that work, Peck identified three key concepts related to efforts to improve schools: (1) Certain factors consistently matter in school reform, including race, ethnicity, and poverty; politics and power; and trust between reformers and those undergoing reform. (2) The outsider issue, in which external reformers assert good intentions, while established locals discern questionable motives. (3) School reform operates in a cycle in which high hopes typically meet with disappointing results and repeat.

The authors also examine the history of reading reform efforts and Bill's experiences in light of several lasting school reform tensions that Peck (2017) identified, including:

- schools affect communities versus communities affect schools,
- the pursuit of social justice through reform versus the pursuit of financial returns through reform, and
- small-scale reforms versus large-scale reforms.

Finally, the authors discuss the lessons they learned from studying about and participating in five decades of reading instruction and reform.

The Outsider Issue

This factor played out in several different settings where Bill worked. Teaching in the schools of Buffalo, New York, Bill was an outsider by race as well as class in the urban community where he worked. Throughout chapter 2, he describes the challenges he faced in engaging students and managing his classroom effectively, noting that "survival was the order of the day." When he joined the Follow Through program, however, he did discover more viable professional supports and community connections, thus mitigating some of the outsider effects.

The outsider issue carried over to Bill's next assignment in the CT program in Vermont, where he entered as a stranger in the sense of not only the rural geographic setting but the nature of the work guiding and supporting adult teachers. Add to that, he was a behaviorist in a district that was concerned enough about that approach to ask him whether he was a "Skinnerian" at his interview.

In the CT program, Bill benefited from and appreciated the "concrete guidelines for what to do" when teaching children with disabilities to read. In this way, being part of a well-structured, highly focused program, this time based on a behavioral approach, helped address the effects of being an outsider. Bill adapted to being an outsider in part by bringing to his schools what he had found generally lacking in Buffalo: a specific plan for improving student behavior and achievement.

As Bill described in chapter 4, the outsider issue emerged in full force as he and Mary attempted to transport their PRIDE model that had experienced success in three schools an hour from the university campus where he taught to a school district in the Southeast. From his first meeting with the teachers on a Friday afternoon, when teachers jumped over a rope barrier to move farther away from Bill as he introduced the plan, it was clear that he and his project director Mary would not enjoy an easy voyage as they sought to implement their program in forty schools.

Bill's organization was understaffed for such a large undertaking. They could provide dedicated service at the three schools in PRIDE, but were stretched thin to provide such careful, constant interventions and support across dozens and dozens of schools. In addition, district realities such as administration changes, teacher pushback, and principal disinterest complicated the implementation process. Yet, in the end, the outsider problem remained, as evidenced by the new superintendent, who yelled out at an opening program for the year, "This year we are getting rid of those damned Yankee reading folks."

Trust

The negative reaction from the teachers and administrators toward Bill's scale-up reform project suggests how difficult it is to develop and sustain trust between reformers and those undergoing reform. Trust can be a challenge in these top-down reform situations due to the politicized nature of educational policy and change. Distrust can serve as a means to prevent unwanted change or to undermine a reform to which individuals might be philosophically opposed.

Prepackaged reading programs remain in common use in schools and tend to accompany top-down change. Such programs can be seen by teachers as a lack of trust in their expertise. Project PRIDE, while largely prepackaged, generated impressive results, especially in one school, through the continuous, positive support provided by Bill and his project director. That support led to teachers feeling pride in what they were accomplishing, which, in turn, continuously nurtured their trust in Bill's program.

It was in the realm "beyond" the three PRIDE schools, however, where trust truly became an issue. For example, the district's literacy director remained a steadfast "balanced literacy" advocate and seemed unwilling or unable to support PRIDE and its "phonics when necessary" approach, even in face of the marked test score improvements that PRIDE created.

One wonders whether a sufficient level of trust could ever be established in order to turn such a true doubter of any approach that included systematic, explicit phonics into a believer. Of course in the scale-up project, Bill was unable to establish trust, at least in part because of the lack of support staff for the schools involved.

Reform as a Cycle

Experienced educators recognize the familiar idea that if you do not like a particular reform that is being introduced, that is okay, because another one will be along soon to replace it. Evidence of a reform cycle that occurs in reading instruction is the pendulum that swings between phonics and meaning-emphasis approaches as the favored approach during an era. Bill even mentioned that in presentations about their project when they would show a slide with a red line drawn through it and the caption, "No More Pendulum."

Yet, cycles and pendulums are very difficult to stop, so what can seem like a new approach today is often merely an old approach recycled from the past. As Bill noted when he returned to urban schools with the PRIDE project, very little had apparently changed from when he was a teacher in Buffalo in the 1970s. Even PRIDE, as successful as it was, succumbed over time to a new administration's desire for a new reform that they could call their own. It is worrisome that the cycle of reform, more than any reform itself, endures, just as the pendulum swings even as we try to stop it. The tensions at play as Bill attempted to engage in reading instruction and reform are now considered.

Schools and Communities

In the interplay between schools and communities that Bill experienced at different stages, he was encountering one of the enduring tensions of school reform: schools affect communities and communities affect schools. In Buffalo, he consciously worked against the Coleman study's assertion that schools could not help children overcome the effects of poverty.

Instead, he prided himself on writing notes home, making phone calls, and visiting students' homes to support his students. Perhaps that was at least part of the reason he found most of his parents supportive. Bill also noted that community organizers, such as those affiliated with Saul Alinsky, were active near his school. Such connections suggested how healthy relationships between schools and communities are possible.

Nonetheless, Bill also recognized that the effects of poverty on student reading achievement "cannot be ignored." Recall his comparing his task as a teacher to entering a town after a hurricane had hit, thinking, "Where do I start?" Bill also recalled his frustration with a situation in which his paraprofessional, a member of the surrounding community, "seemed to identify more with the students than me, talking and fooling with some of the students while I was teaching." Thus, the tension between schools and communities also resonated in Bill's practice.

Social Justice and Vendor Profit

Bill's experiences shed light on another common reform issue: the potential tension at play between the pursuit of educational reform for social justice versus the pursuit of educational reform for vendor profit. For example, as Russakoff (2015) reported regarding Newark's recent experience with school reform, "A Newark school leader described the situation as the 'school failure industry.' Everyone's getting paid, and Raheem still can't read" (pp. 71–2).

Also, as dramatically demonstrated in RF, even the appearance of a conflict of interest can undermine an otherwise good-faith effort.

Clearly, over the years, Bill benefited from his work as an educator in a number of tangible ways: two master's degrees and a Ph.D., all paid for by the federal government, a lifetime of job security, royalties from textbook writing, and a nice pension. Besides, the products he used as well as the programs he helped operate generated significant financial returns for commercial companies.

For example, Bill used the ubiquitous basal readers in his classrooms, explaining that they were "a life-saver since it readily filled my information void." He also has advocated for the use of Direct Instruction materials which are published by a known commercial concern, SRA. Add to that, early in his career as a professor, he contracted with local schools to provide one-day professional development in-services. These one-time, "Thank You and God Bless You" sessions were sarcastically referred to by Bill and his colleagues as "prostitution."

Nonetheless, despite all of this, Bill's writing makes it clear that he was also motivated by a sincere, abiding desire to improve the life chances of children by equipping them with the reading skills they needed to pursue so many academic and life goals. His mission included later professional development efforts that were made more meaningful and productive by being collaborative and long-term. In the case of Project PRIDE, his efforts resulted in meaningful reading gains for children.

While money can certainly corrupt, in education and all professions, corruption is not necessarily a fait accompli. If done appropriately, an entrepreneurial approach can be a win for the children and the contractor. It's not the financial arrangement per se that is the problem, but the manner in which it is carried out.

Large Scale versus Small Scale

At its most basic level, education is a small-scale undertaking: a teacher working in a classroom with a group of students. As researchers such as Payne (2008) have noted, problems emerge and then persist as we try to take what works in one research study or one classroom (or even one school) and expand the reach of that reform program into other schools, districts, and states. The larger the scale of the reform implementation, the more likely it is to depart from its original design.

Large-scale reform is also likely to take on characteristics of a top-down imposition in which teachers are expected to act as passive recipients rather than active collaborators. As discussed about trust, teachers can greet such top-down reforms with evident skepticism (if not open hostility), which complicates the reform's potential to bring about positive change.

Bill's career helps illustrate what we might call an "arc of intervention" that spans from small scale to large scale. While teaching in Buffalo, he was most focused on finding and developing instructional practices that proved effective in his own classroom. To do so, he relied on a combination of individual experimentation and group problem-solving (as well as commiseration) with colleagues. This enabled Bill to identify potentially successful approaches for meeting the needs of particular students in a particular urban community.

In his CT role in Vermont, he helped equip teachers with skills and strategies that they could apply in their own classrooms. Importantly, however, he approached this work as a collaborator, which helped ensure teachers were more likely to accept and adapt as necessary the instructional techniques he presented. Still, there were limits as to how far teachers would go to change the limits exacerbated by Bill's lack of political leverage.

As Bill progressed to creating grant-funded reading interventions while serving as a professor, he found the most success with the PRIDE program that worked well in three schools. What was manageable, effective, and teacher-connected in a small number of schools, however, became, unfortunately, dispersed, unwieldy, and teacher-distant when applied to a far larger number of schools in a district in the Southeast. In the end, Bill's career's "arc of intervention" suggests how the larger the scale, the more difficult the reform effort.

FIVE LESSONS FROM FIVE DECADES OF READING INSTRUCTION AND REFORM

Here are the five lessons that the authors learned from studying about and participating in five decades of reading instruction and reform.

1. *We need to prepare teachers to deliver reading instruction across a range of student needs, using instruction that varies along a continuum of intensities*

One conclusion that can be drawn from Bill's decades of teaching experience is that teachers need to be better prepared to teach children to read who are at risk due to poverty, have a disability, or are English learners. As an elementary school teacher in Buffalo, despite a master's degree in a major that read "urban education" on his transcript, Bill's attempts to teach his students to read were largely unsuccessful.

As a special education consulting teacher in Vermont, Bill finally learned what he needed to do to teach children at risk to read, but encountered general education teachers unprepared to use such methods and often unwilling to acquire them. Bill had to depend on pulling students out of their classrooms and training paraprofessionals to provide the systematic, explicit reading instruction they needed.

The saga continued with Bill's experience as a teacher educator, where he found a seemingly impenetrable ideological barrier between him and his colleagues in special education and the literacy professors who were a part of general education teacher education. While Bill was able to prepare his future special educators with the skills they needed, future general education teachers who were to receive the next generation of students at risk remained unprepared to do so. Finally, Bill attained a measure of success meeting the needs of urban students using a multitiered approach only to have it discontinued by district administrators who were philosophically opposed.

The field urgently needs to agree on a continuum of reading teaching methods needed to meet the range of students faced by teachers in our schools. As a part of this discussion, educators on the more naturalistic side of the instructional continuum need to accept and accommodate levels of systematic and explicit instruction that many of them may have, in the past, dismissed as unnecessary, and maybe even harmful. On the other hand, those on the systematic, explicit, "science of reading" side need to, when appropriate, accommodate instruction that is more naturalistic, which, as Bill's experiences suggest, may for them conjure up unflattering images of whole language.

There also needs to be a meeting of the minds concerning assessment, including agreement as to the right mix of more discrete, skill-based assessments along with more holistic measures. Both word identification and comprehension skills need to be represented in an accurate system that can readily monitor progress in the most important reading skills.

There is some evidence to suggest that a model for enabling a more agreeable future already exists. A recent study of teacher preparation (Feng & Sass, 2013) found that general education students performed better when their teachers were certified in both general and special education. Teachers prepared in both general and special education tend to have a greater range of instructional skills, from naturalistic to carefully designed, and less intensive to more intensive.

Programs that prepare teachers to be both general and special educators are nothing new and a number of current teacher education programs are offering special and general education endorsements together (Fallona & Johnson, 2019). However, as shown in Bill's teacher preparation experience as related in chapter 4, literacy professors and special education professors tend to exist in parallel, wholly separate universes. A combined approach such as the dual certification programs described above would require a level of collaboration, agreement, and coordination not often seen in higher education generally nor teacher education specifically.

The ultimate goal is to empower teachers to meet a range of student needs, but it can only work if it can be realistically and effectively carried out within a typical classroom setting. Otherwise, students with special needs may end up in classrooms that don't meet their needs. This caution is particularly relevant given evidence to suggest that current teacher preparation programs may not be covering reading content adequately (Ross, 2018), and multitiered programs are hard to carry out with the fidelity needed to meet a range of student needs (Gersten et al., 2017).

2. *In preparing teachers to teach reading, we need better structured and more effective collaborations between higher education institutions and K-5 schools*

As recounted in chapter 4, over the course of Bill's career the coordination between coursework and clinical settings remained problematic. This situation was in part due to the fact that at both of his universities selection of clinical sites and supervision within those sites were delegated to adjuncts. Professors played a limited role, apparently so they would have more time to pursue their research agendas. Such a system fosters major gaps between what is covered in on-campus classes and what students can practice in their clinical settings.

Bill was able to engage in several efforts to better align methods, classes, and clinicals, the most successful being when he placed his students with teachers who had been trained to deliver multitier reading through his federal model demonstration grant. As mentioned in chapter 4, that was the only time in his entire career as a teacher educator that he was able to attain a real synergy between campus and field settings.

Future efforts are needed to better coordinate campus and field sites. Certainly, literacy and special education classes need to be better coordinated so that *all* teachers are capable of meeting the needs of a range of students. In addition, the coordination effort required between literacy and special education should involve classroom teachers, both to verify the relevance of the arrived at curricula and to identify needed areas of professional development.

Last, what has been a perennial tension between professors' teaching and research responsibilities should not be allowed to perpetuate the divide between coursework and field practices. Efforts should be undertaken to more directly tie professors' reward systems to research and the development of evidence-based clinical operations.

3. *Reform that is smaller scale, local, and collaborative has the greatest chance for success*

The history of reading reform in general and Bill's experiences with it in particular reveals the challenges reformers face when "scaling-up" initiatives that have demonstrated success in a small number of classrooms or a single school. What works in one school rarely works in 100 or 1,000. Efforts to expand are often made from afar, impeding the building of genuine relationships with the educators undergoing change and making it difficult to respond to problems as they arise.

Distance, in essence, can lead to resistance to the intended reform from the local educators tasked with actual implementation. As those local educators build greater mistrust of reform intentions, their sense that adoption of the initiatives is a top-down mandate only grows.

Given these conditions, it is essential that those hoping to improve reading and reading instruction keep in mind that smaller scale, local, and collaborative efforts may have the best chance to generate positive results. Hence, future reformers might heed this piece of advice: if you are stepping on an airplane to fly somewhere to implement a school reform design, it probably will not work, unless of course you are planning to stay in the community on a permanent basis.

4. *Take "PRIDE" in the best things that we do in reading reform*

It is clear from our study of and engagement in reforming reading instruction over the past fifty years that doing so successfully is a difficult process. Mirroring the larger story of school reform in the United States (Tyack & Cuban, 1995), time and again reading initiatives and programs that promised significant change failed to deliver meaningful, lasting results. Moreover, the ongoing, polarizing rhetorical war between meaning-based and phonics advocates has created a policy environment characteristic of an educational pendulum in which implemented programs have swung from one instructional extreme to another.

In such circumstances, educators learned little that they might carry forward. Instead, like surfers in the ocean, they were left to expect a new reform wave to emerge inevitably and hope to ride it successfully. There is fresh evidence that we are now engaging in yet another chapter in these seemingly endless reading wars (Gabriel, 2020; Shanahan, 2019), with the "science of reading" professionals advocating for phonics as of this writing. (Seidenberg, 2014).

Given this broader context of disappointment, it is important to emphasize that engaging in successful reform of reading instruction is possible. The best evidence from Bill's career is his Project PRIDE experience. It consisted of a small-scale expansion of a professional development intervention in one school that was funded at all levels with supplementary federal grant assistance. The scale-up was to three schools that were within driving distance of Bill and his project manager, which ensured they could remain meaningfully involved in all aspects of the project consistently. Bill and Mary also ensured that teachers were partners in implementation through careful and constant collaboration.

The program's positive academic results at the school in the form of students' year-end test score improvement as well as its positive impact on overall school culture offer direct testimony to its success. Though the program did not last in the particular district in which it was implemented, it did, through its design and scale, offer the potential for replication. Project PRIDE, in essence, offered a necessary antidote to what Bill called, "Thank You and God Bless You" professional development.

5. *There is no reform panacea, but doing nothing is not an option*

After five decades of reading reform and research, the authors regretfully, but admittedly with some relief, have concluded that the search for the "best" method of teaching reading is a futile one. It is also time to end the practice of "death by interpretation," whereby research results are discounted if they conflict with one's reading philosophy. If reading experts in the 1960s and 1970s had only heeded the research at the time and earnestly tackled the problem of how to incorporate both systematic, explicit phonics and comprehension into a total reading program, we may have been able to avoid the decades of reading wars that followed.

In truth, the reading glass is both half empty *and* half full. The panacea we all seek is an imperfect one but seek it we must. We need to proceed with humility and with a sense of skepticism that transcends our individual biases. We need to make an all-out effort to verify as carefully as we can the results of our efforts while making a solid commitment to learning as we go, including from each other.

If the years after RF have taught us anything, it's that simply declaring instruction "balanced" or "scientific" is not enough. A viable start toward reconciliation would be for researchers, practitioners, and policymakers to gather, perhaps with federal support, to arrive at a working definition of effective reading instruction, taking into account both word analysis and comprehension-based emphases.

Commercial reading programs, long a major part of classroom reading instruction, could play an important role in bringing to fruition whatever conception of reading is ultimately agreed upon. Basal readers and prescribed reading programs don't necessarily have to undermine teacher autonomy, but can play an active role in stimulating teacher professionalism and self-efficacy (Ball & Cohen, 1996).

Last, an effective reading future involves more than formulating policy and selecting effective teaching practices and programs. The future requires an understanding of the process of policy implementation, and acting upon that understanding, collaboratively, and across disciplines.

CONCLUSION: FINDING HOPE IN THE "RADICAL MIDDLE" AND GETTING OFF THE PENDULUM

In this book, the authors have strived to make sense of over a half century of reading instruction and reform by considering the larger picture, in the form of policy debates and major reading initiatives, and the smaller picture, in the form of the experiences of Bill Bursuck as he navigated various educational settings. In concluding, the authors return to where the book began by revisiting the opening vignettes in the Introduction.

In Bill's vignette, he provided personal insight into the growth and success of the Project PRIDE program, but also expressed concern about its demise and, eventually, the erosion of reading gains in the three schools. Craig Peck, in turn, recalled his time serving as a high-school social studies teacher in an urban California setting, where his affinity for his students was matched with concern that he had few workable options to improve the educational chances of those students in the class who were far below grade level in reading.

The vignettes, like the larger book, help illustrate the complexity of reading instruction and reform. On the one hand, there is the disappointing if not debilitating sense of unfulfilled expectations. Even as the authors endeavored to provide educational stepping stones to students, they struggled against the rising tides of schooling dysfunction and social challenges that could so easily frustrate their best-intended efforts.

On the other hand, the authors' vignettes and experiences as well as the history of reading instruction and reform demonstrate the fundamentally democratic idea that hope has played and continues to play in propelling educational reform. Indeed, a central element that resonates in Bill's recounting of his career is hope. There was hope that drove his desire to work in an urban context through the Teacher Corps and hope in his decision to join the CT program and work with students with disabilities.

There was the hope that compelled him to find ways to bring about better reading outcomes for his students by seeking opportunities for grant funding. The type of hope that fueled Bill's career path and work, in fact, continues to fuel broader social efforts to improve reading instruction and academic outcomes.

In closing, then, the authors want to focus on the hope that they have seen and do see as representing the potential for positive reform in reading instruction. Most importantly, they find hope in the idea that there is what Pearson (2012) called a "radical middle" that rests as a fair, useful space in between the forceful poles of the reading wars. The authors believe there is plenty of room under this tent to provide students with the skills and knowledge base they need to become life-long readers who can understand, appreciate, and critique what they read.

All of us need to recognize that naturalistic, meaning-based or systematic, explicit teaching is neither the sole answer nor the sole problem. By encouraging teachers, principals, university instructors, and professional development providers to "hug the middle" (Cuban, 2009), we can offer the chance for future and current reading teachers to employ a wider range of instructional approaches that will remain at their disposal. It is not systematic, explicit phonics only; it is systematic, explicit phonics as needed. It is not comprehension-based instruction only; it is comprehension-based instruction for all in addition to whatever type of code-based teaching may be necessary.

In this way, teachers can be equipped with various tools for teaching reading, toolkits that they can use at their discretion, rather than insisting that there is only one tool that works in every context. Of course, all instructional decisions need to be made based on the best student performance data possible, encompassing as broad a spectrum of reading goals as is feasible.

Looking over fifty years of debates, dialogues, and battles over reading instruction, the authors believe a middle path is the best path forward for realizing meaningful change. The middle path need not be watered down, milquetoast, a halfway point. Rather, the middle can be three dimensional and extreme, a position that requires the hard work of entering into brave discussions without condemning the other persons' motivations (Burke, Personal Communication, January 11, 2021). Though this path offers no panacea, it does offer the best bet toward getting off the pendulum and attaining a better future.

References

Ball, D. L., & Cohen, D. K. (1996). Reform by the book: What is-or might be-the role of curriculum materials in teacher learning and instructional reform? *Educational Researcher, 25*(9), 6–8, 14.

Bean, R. M., Dole, J. A., Nelson, K. L., Belcastro, E. G., & Zigmond, N. (2015). The sustainability of a national reading reform initiative in two states. *Reading and Writing Quarterly, 31*(1), 30–55, doi: 10.1080/10573569.2013.857947.

Beck, I. L. (2010). Half-full or half-empty. *Journal of Literacy Research, 42,* 94–99.

Bursuck, W. D., & Damer, M. (2015). *Teaching reading to students who are at risk or have disabilities: A multi-tier, RTI approach.* New York, NY: Pearson Higher Education.

Carnine, D., Silbert, J., Kame'enui, E. J., Slocum, T. A., & Travers, P. A. (2017). *Direct Instruction Reading* (6th ed.). Boston, MA: Pearson.

Castles, A., Rastle, K., & Nation, K. (2018). Corrigendum: Ending the reading wars: Reading acquisition from novice to expert. *Psychological Science in the Public Interest, 19,* 5–51. doi:10.1177/1529100618772271

Chall, J. S. (1967). *Learning to read: The great debate.* New York, NY: McGraw Hill.

Cleaver, E. (1991). *Soul on ice.* New York, NY: Delta Trade Paperbacks.

Coburn, C. E., Pearson, P. D., & Woulfin, S. (2011). Reading policy in the era of accountability. In M. Kamil, P. D. Pearson, E. B. Moje, & P. P. Afflerbach (Eds.), *Handbook of Reading Research Volume IV,* 587–619. New York, NY: Routledge.

Coburn, C. E., & Woulfin, S. L. (2012). Reading coaches and the relationship between policy and practice. *Reading Research Quarterly, 47*(1), 5–30.

Cooper, H. (2005). Reading between the lines: Observations on the report of the National Reading panel and its critics. *Phi Delta Kappan, 86*(6), 456–461.

Cuban, L. (1974). Reform by fiat: The Clark plan in Washington, 1970–1972. *Urban Education, 9*(1), 8–34.

Cuban, L. (2009). *Hugging the middle.* New York, NY: Teachers College Press

Dillon, S. (2008, May 1). Reading program is called ineffective. *New York Times.* Retrieved from https://www.nytimes.com/2008/05/01/washington/01cnd-read.html

Durkin, D. (1978-79). What classroom observations reveal about reading comprehension instruction. *Reading Research Quarterly, 14*(4), 481–533.

Edmonds, R. (1979). Effective schools for the urban poor. *Educational Leadership, 37*(1), 15–24.

Ehri, L.C. (2020). The science of learning to read words. *Reading Research Quarterly, 55*(1), 45–60.

Elliott, J.G. (2020). It's time to be scientific about dyslexia. *Reading Research Quarterly, 55*(1), 61–75

Engelmann, S. (2007). *Teaching needy kids in our backward system.* Eugene, OR: ADI Press.

Fallona, C., & Johnson, A. (2019). *Approaches to "Grow Your Own" and dual general and special education certification.* Gorham, Maine: University of Southern Maine; Center for Education Policy, Applied Research & Evaluation.

Feng, L., & Sass, T. R. (2013). What makes special-education teachers special? Teacher training and achievement of students with disabilities. *Economics of Education Review, 36*(C), 122–134.

Fletcher, J. M., Lyon, G. R., Fuchs, L. S., & Barnes, M. A. (2019). *Learning Disabilities: From Identification to Intervention* (2nd ed.). New York, NY: Guilford Press.

Freire, P. (2013). *Education for critical consciousness.* London, England: Bloomsbury Academic.

Friend, M., & Bursuck, W. D. (2019). *Including students with special needs: A practical guide for classroom teachers* (9th ed.). Boston, MA: Pearson.

Fuchs, D., & Fuchs, L. S. (2017). Critique of the national evaluation of response to intervention: A case for simpler frameworks. *Exceptional Children, 83*(3), 255–268. doi:10.1177/001402917693580.

Gabriel, R. (2020). The future of the science of reading. *The Reading Teacher, 74*(1), 11–18.

Gamse, B. C., Jacob, R. T., Horst, M., Boulay, B., & Unlu, F. (2008). *Reading First impact study final report.* National Center for Evaluation and Regional Assistance, Institute of Education Sciences. Washington, DC: U.S. Department of Education (NCEE 2009-4038).

Gersten, R., Jayanthi, M., & Dimino, J. (2017). Too much too soon? Unanswered questions from national response to intervention evaluation. *Exceptional Children, 83*(3), 244–254. doi:10.1177/0014402917692847

Glenn, D. (2007, February 2). Reading for profit. *Chronicle of Higher Education,* pp. A8–A13.

Goodman, K. S. (2006). *DIBELS: What it is. What it does.* Portsmouth, NH: Heinemann.

Goodman, K. S., & Goodman, Y. M. (1977). Learning about psycholinguistic processes by analyzing oral reading. *Harvard Educational Review, 47,* 317–333.

Hindman, A.H., Morrison, F.J., Connor, C.M., & Connor, J.A. (2020). Bringing the science of reading to preservice elementary teachers: Tools that bridge research and practice. *Reading Research Quarterly, 55*(1), 197–206.

Hanushek, E. A., Peterson, P. E., Talpey, L. M., & Woessmann, L. (2019). The achievement gap fails to close. *Education Next, 19*(3), Retrieved from: https://www.educationnext.org/achievement-gap-fails-close-half-century-testing-shows-persistent-divide/

Heward, W., Damer, M., & Wood, C. (2004 April) *Faux Fonics: A behavioral and instructional analysis of phonics activities that aren't*. Boston, MA: Association for Behavior Analysis International.

Hildreth, G. (1958). *Teaching reading*. New York, NY: Holt, Rinehart and Winston.

Jennings, J. L., Deming, D., Jencks, C., Lopuch, M., & Schuler, M. (2015). Do differences in school quality matters more than we thought? New evidence on educational opportunity in the Twenty-First Century. *Sociology of Education, 88*(1), 56–82. doi::10.1177/0038040714562006.

Johnston, V. (2019). Dyslexia: What reading teachers need to know. *The Reading Teacher, 73*(3), 339–346.

Kamil, M. L. (2015). Relevance of models for common core state standards. In P. David Pearson and E. H. Hiebert (Eds), *Research-based practices for teaching common core literacy* (pp. 41–56). New York, NY: Teachers College, Columbia University.

Kim, J. S. (2008). Research and the reading wars. In F. M. Hess (Ed.), *When Research Matters: How Scholarship Influences Education Policy* (pp. 89–111). Cambridge, MA: Harvard Education Press.

Kozol, J. (1980). *Prisoners of silence: Breaking the bonds of adult illiteracy in the United States*. New York, NY: Continuum Publishing Corporation.

Lyon, G. R., & Fletcher, J. M. (2001, Summer). Early warning system: How to prevent reading disabilities. *Education Matters, 1*(2), 22–29.

Meisinger, E. B., Bradley, B. A., Schwanenflugel, P. J., Kuhn, M. R., & Morris, R. D. (2009). Myth and reality of the word caller: the relation between teacher nominations and prevalence among elementary school children. *School Psychology Quarterly, 24*(3), 147–150.

Moats, L. (2020). *Speech to print: Language essentials for teachers* (3rd ed.). Baltimore, MD: Paul Brookes.

National Reading Panel. (2000). *Teaching children to read: An evidence-based assessment of the scientific research literature on reading and its implications for reading instruction*. Washington, DC: National Institute of Child Health and Human Development.

Parker, J. T. (1964). Frontal attack on illiteracy. In I. Isenberg (Ed.), *The drive against illiteracy* (pp. 154–156). New York, NY: HW Wilson Company.

Payne, C. M. (2008). *So much reform so little change: The persistence of failure in urban schools*. Cambridge, MA: Harvard Education Press.

Pearson, P. D. (1999). *Reading in the Twentieth Century*. Retrieved from http://www.ciera.org/library/archive/2001-08/200108.htm.

Pearson. P.D. (2000). *Reading in the twentieth century* (Report no. ED479530). Ann Arbor, MI: CIERA/University of Michigan.

Pearson, P. D. (2004). The reading wars. *Educational Policy, 18*(1), 216–252.

Pearson, P. D. (2010). Reading First: Hard to live with-or without. *Journal of Literacy Research, 42*, 100–108.

Pearson, P. D. (2012). Point of View: Life in the radical middle. In R. F. Flippo (Ed.), *Reading Researchers in Search of Common Ground* (pp. 99–106). New York: Routledge.

Peck, C. (2017, March). *Urban school reform in the United States*. Oxford Encyclopedia of Education. Retrieved from https://oxfordre.com/education/view/10.1093/acrefore/9780190264093.001.0001/acrefore-9780190264093-e-27

Reed, W. O. (1964). Relating reality to education. In I. Isenberg (Ed.), *The drive against illiteracy* (pp. 154–156). New York, NY: HW Wilson Company.

Rogers, C. R. (1968). Learning to be free. In G. Natchez (Ed.), *Children with reading problems: Classic and contemporary issues in reading disability* (pp. 427–432). New York, NY: Basic Books.

Ross, E. (2018). *NCTQ data burst: Strengthening reading instruction through better preparation of elementary and special education teachers.* Washington, DC: National Council on Teacher Quality.

Russakoff, D. (2015). *The Prize.* Boston, MA: Houghton Mifflin Harcourt.

Seidenberg, M. (2014). *Language at the speed of sight.* New York, NY: Basic Books-Hatchett Book Group.

Seidenberg, M. S., Borkenhagen, M. C., & Kearns, D. M. (2020). Lost in translation? Challenges in connecting reading science and educational practice. *Reading Research Quarterly, 55*(1), 119–130.

Shanahan, T. (2003). Research-based reading instruction: Myths about the National Reading panel Report. *The Reading Teacher, 56*(7), 646–655.

Shanahan, T. (2019). *Reading wars: What's a literacy coach to do?* Retrieved from https://shanahanonliteracy.com/blog/have-the-reading-wars-become-research-wars

Shannon, P. (1988). *Broken promises: Reading instruction in Twentieth-century America.* Granby, MA: Bergin & Garvey Publishers.

Shaywitz, S., Morris, M., & Shaywitz, B. (2008). The education of dyslexic children from childhood to young adulthood. *Annual Review of Psychology, 59*, 451–475.

Smith, F. (1971). *Understanding reading: A psycholinguistic analysis of reading and learning to read.* New York, NY: Holt, Rinehart & Winston.

Snow, C. E., Burns, M. S., & Griffin, P. (1998). *Preventing reading difficulties in young children.* Washington, DC: National Research Council.

Stahl, S. A. (1999). Why innovations come and go (and mostly go): The case of whole language. *Educational Researcher, 28*(8), 13–22.

Stedman, L. C., & Kaestle, C. F. (1988). Literacy and reading performance in the United States from 1880 to the present. In C. F. Kaestle, H. Damon-Moore, L. C. Stedman, K. Tinsley, & W. V. Trollinger, Jr. (Eds.), *Literacy in the United States: Readers and reading since 1880* (pp. 75–128). New Haven, CT: Yale University Press.

Steinbeck, J. (1976). The acts of King Arthur and his noble knights: Introduction to his translation of *Le Morte d'Arthur*. In *The Winchester manuscripts of Thomas Malory & Other Sources* (pp. 3–4). Portsmouth, NH: Heinemann Publishing Company.

Stern (2008). *Too good to last: The true story of reading first.* New York, NY: Fordham Institute.

Tyack, D., & Cuban, L. (1995). *Tinkering with utopia: A century of public school reform.* Cambridge, MA: Harvard University Press

Wallace, J. (n.d.). Carol Moseley Braun, former U.S. Senator & U.S. Ambassador to New Zealand. *The Yale Center for Dyslexia and Creativity.* Retrieved from https://dyslexia.yale.edu/story/carol-moseley-braun-2/

Whitehurst, G. (2003, September 10). Interview: Evidence-based education science and the challenge of learning to read [Electronic version]. David Boulton. retrieved from http://www.childrenofthecode.org/interviews/whitehurst.htm

About the Authors

Dr. William D. Bursuck is professor emeritus at the University of North Carolina at Greensboro. He has been interested in reading instruction ever since an unsuccessful stint teaching reading as a Teacher Corps intern and an urban elementary school teacher in Buffalo, New York. In search of answers to the literacy puzzle, Dr. Bursuck first pursued a master's degree in special education at the University of Vermont and spent three years as a special education consulting teacher in six rural elementary schools. Following that he obtained his Ph.D. in special education from the University of Illinois at Urbana-Champaign. Up until his retirement in 2014, Dr. Bursuck was involved in preparing special and general education teachers to employ the systematic and explicit instruction needed to effectively teach students at risk or who have disabilities to read and perform other essential academic skills.

Dr. Bursuck (with Dr. Marilyn Friend) is the author of the popular text *Including Students with Special Needs: A Practical Guide for Teachers*, which is now in its eighth edition. He has been the principal investigator for over a million dollars in federal grants, including Project PRIDE, a federally funded model-demonstration research grant that pioneered multitier practices for teaching reading. Based on that project, Dr. Bursuck published (with Mary Damer) a reading methods text, *Teaching Reading to Students Who Are At Risk or Have Disabilities: A Multi-Tier, RTI Approach*.

Dr. Craig Peck joined the UNC Greensboro faculty in 2007. Previously, he worked in several positions in K-12 education, including serving as a public high-school principal in New York City. He received his Ph.D. in History of Education from Stanford University in 2001. At UNC Greensboro, he has worked collaboratively with department colleagues to develop new initiatives intended to help prepare excellent school leaders. From 2011 to 2014, he co-developed and helped manage a $6.2 million grant-funded initiative to train future leaders of high-need schools in four local, demographically diverse school districts. He teaches courses related to educational leadership, urban education, school reform, and doctoral studies.

Dr. Peck's research interests include principals, urban schools, and educational reform since the 1960s. His research has appeared in journals such as *Educational Administration Quarterly*, *Education and Urban Society*, *Teachers College Record*, and *Urban Education*. He serves as a mentor in programs such as the Barbara Jackson Scholar Network of the University Council for Educational Administration (UCEA) and the African American Male Initiative at Wiley Elementary School in Greensboro.

www.ingramcontent.com/pod-product-compliance
Lightning Source LLC
Chambersburg PA
CBHW022016300426
44117CB00005B/216